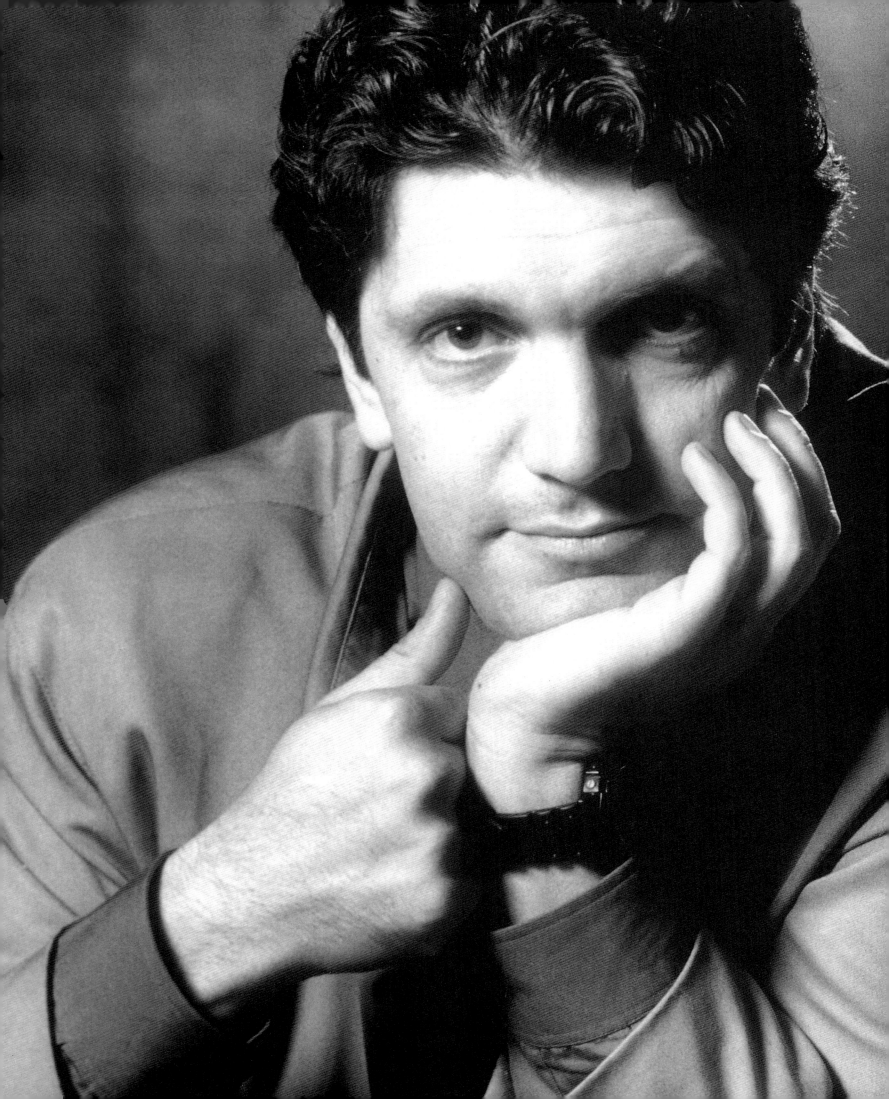

ALFREDO ARRIBAS ARQUITECTOS ASOCIADOS

Werke/Works 1991-95

Einführung und Projektbeschreibungen/Introduction and Project Descriptions

Georg-Christof Bertsch

Mit Texten von/With texts by

Hellmut Seemann

Enric Miralles

Wasmuth Verlag

Dieser Katalog erscheint anläßlich der Ausstellung
»Ich schlafe nie« Alfredo Arribas - eine Monografie seiner Arbeiten 1991-96

Eine Ausstellung im Karmeliterkloster, Frankfurt am Main
anläßlich der Design Horizonte 1995
1.-24.9.1995

Eine Ausstellung der **Annette Bertsch GmbH**, Frankfurt am Main
in Zusammenarbeit mit:
   Dr. Klaus Klemp, Amt für Wissenschaft und Kunst der Stadt Frankfurt

Kurator der Ausstellung:
   Georg-Christof Bertsch

Projektleitung:
   Alexandra Reinhold

Ausstellungsbau:
   Ingo Fabian nach Entwürfen von **Alfredo Arribas**

Impressum

© 1995 by **Ernst Wasmuth Verlag**, Tübingen, Berlin
und **Annette Bertsch GmbH**, Frankfurt am Main

ISBN 3-8030-3074-9

Grafikdesign des Kataloges:
   Annette Bertsch

Übersetzungen:
   Dr. Jeremy Gaines
   Oliver Remme
   Rebecca L. Wallach

Gedruckt von:
   Druckerei und Verlag Otto Lembeck, Frankfurt am Main

Dieser Katalogband erscheint als Folgeband der Werkmonografie
»Alfredo Arribas Arquitectos Asociados Architecture and Design 1986-92«,
Ernst Wasmuth Verlag, Tübingen, Berlin, 1993

Diese Publikation wurde ermöglicht durch die großzügige Unterstützung
des GRUNDWERT-FONDS der DEGI Deutsche Gesellschaft für Immobilienfonds mbH, Frankfurt am Main.

RES PUBLICA

Architektur im Zeitalter von Virtual Reality und Cyberspace, vor dem Hintergrund von Konsumüberdruß und brachialer Marketinggewalt der Medienindustrie ist zwangsläufig Bestandteil von Imagestrategien - im Wettrennen um wirtschaftliches Überleben. Japan hat es - im negativen Sinne - vorgemacht: Gebäude von Stararchitekten, die zuerst dem Image der Firma dienen und erst in zweiter Linie funktionalen Gesichtspunkten gehorchen. Gebäude überdies, die nicht einen Bruchteil des innerstädtischen Grundstückswertes haben und eher zum Bereich der ephemeren Architektur (Messebau, Bühnenbau) gehören als zu dem Schaffen einer Stadt mit sozialem Bewußtsein.

Robert Venturi hat 1972 mit seinem »Learning from Las Vegas« den Startschuß gegeben für die Integration von Pop-Elementen in die Architektur. Für Arribas bedeutet dies den Einsatz von Images, Atmosphären und Bildern aus dem Arsenal des kollektiven Wissens und Unterbewußten: Pop im Sinne von Allgemeinverständlichkeit. Er bewegt sich daher immer im Bereich der res publica und nicht umsonst war die frühe Begegnung mit Leon Krier einer der Initialmomente für sein architektonisches Schaffen.

Res publica wird hier aber nicht mehr als Schaffen von großen Plätzen, der Öffentlichkeit der Antike und noch des 19. Jh. begriffen, sondern als Zugriff auf die neuen sozialen Zentren: Diskotheken, Konzerthallen, Kinos, mit ihren spezifischen Umgangsformen und Kontaktmöglichkeiten. Diese Vorgehensweise, die die Gestaltung von Bars und Restaurants auf eine »städtebauliche« Ebene hebt, unterscheidet Arribas von vielen stilistisch vergleichbaren Kollegen. Seine Jahre als Dozent für Architekturtheorie an der Escuela Superior de Arquitectura in Barcelona haben ihm das Wissen verschafft, mit dem er seit Beginn der 90er Jahre immer größere Projekte bewältigt. Das wohl prägnanteste Merkmal ist seine Liebe zu den atmosphärischen Details - und seine Ablehnung jeglicher Form von Arroganz gegenüber dem Benutzer.

We are living in era of virtual reality and cyberspace, excessive consumerism and the brute marketing force of the media industry. In such a context, architecture has inevitably become a component of image- promoting strategies, a means of staying ahead in the race for economic survival. In Japan, this trend and its negative side-effects have been effectively demonstrated: star architects design buildings which are intended above all to serve company image, with functional aspects playing only a secondary role. Furthermore, the value of such buildings is not even a fraction of what urban property is typically worth. They belong more to the realm of ephemeral architecture (fairground and stage construction) than to building a city with social awareness.

In 1972, Robert Venturi gave the go-ahead for integrating pop elements into architecture with his »Learning from Las Vegas« project. For Arribas, this means using images, atmospheres and images from the arsenal of collective knowledge and the collective unconscious: pop in the sense of being understood by a general public. Thus he always moves within the scope of res publica, and it is no coincidence that is early encounter with Leon Krier was one of the events to pave the way for his subsequent architectural works.

However, res publica is no longer understood as creating large spaces, the »public domain« of antiquity and even of the 19th century, but rather as focusing attention on the new social centers: discotheques, concert halls, and cinemas, each with its specific etiquette, each offering unique opportunities to make contact with others. This approach, which elevated bar and restaurant designto the level of »urban development«, distinguishes Arribas from many of his colleagues who are comparable to him in terms of style. The years he spend as a lecturer in architectural theory at the Escuela Superior de Arquitectura in Barcelona equipped him with the knowledge which he has used since the beginning of the Nineties to master increasingly larger projects. The most characteristic feature is his love of atmospheric detail – and his rejection of any form of arrogance with respect to the user.

Wir möchten uns an dieser Stelle bei dem GRUNDWERT-FONDS der DEGI Deutsche Gesellschaft für Immobilienfonds mbH, Frankfurt am Main bedanken. Ohne dessen großzügige Unterstützung hätte sich dieses Buch nicht realisieren lassen.

We would like to take this opportunity to extend a heartfelt thanks to the GRUNDWERT-FONDS at DEGI Deutsche Gesellschaft für Immobilienfonds mbH in Frankfurt. Without DEGI´s generous support, the publication of this book would not have been possible.

Tailoring is dying out as a profession.

Hellmut Seemann

Tailoring is dying out as a profession. Once upon a time, tailors were the commissioners of social intercourse, mediating between individual and social demands. In the pre-bourgeois world, people wore uniform clothing in keeping with their station in life; only when people became free citizens did they require individual clothing marking off and pointing up the intimate sphere of the body while at the same time making them presentable in decent society. The spontaneous, arbitrariness of »anything goes«, which permits the indifferent ugliness of the political elite as well as the brandname consciousness of the creative elite, is rendering tailors obsolete.

The view that the individual is both the atom and the eternal opponent of the social is an outdated way of looking at things which ceased to be with the victory of mass culture. However, attention must be drawn to the connection which exists between the dreadful cult of turn-of-the-century reformers, either naked or wrapped in flowing sheets, and the polished interiors of art nouveau. For the less clothing is capable of backing up the individual, the more important things such as interiors and spatial scenarios become, as these may be worn as a second skin. Those dependent upon communicative settings are no longer defined as individuals, but rather as the opposite: they are connoisseurs of potentially widely divergent communicative situations, in which they know how to participate. Ambiance is their Ego, design is their virtue.

Alfredo Arribas is a custom tailor of such ambiances. I have had the true pleasure of being able to experience one. Alfredo Arribas exhibited his furniture pieces in the Schirn Kunsthalle rotunda as part of Design Horizonte 1990. It was the first time his work had appeared in Frankfurt. The amazing display of chairs, armchairs and benches (Jane Greystoke) seemed completely out of place on the floor of the concrete barrel like construction. Excellent craftsmanship employing wood, steel and leather gave the person sitting the feeling of complete acceptance.

In those days, the Schirn Café was in a deplorable state. The world »café« is not even really applicable, a fact attributable not least to the people who were running the place, or perhaps one could also say that an impossible space had found the appropriate management. All the same, it was less inner conviction than a profound respect for the favorite toys of his employees that in the end led Christoph Vitali, the Schirn's Director, to invite Alfredo Arribas to conjure up some ideas on redesigning the Schirn Café.

Frankfurt was still terra incognita for Arribas. My fear was that he might simply supply a complete and finished design concept that would then be as permanently out of place as had been his undoubtedly beautiful chairs were in the rotunda. However, not only was this fear unfounded, what happened was exactly contrary to expectation. Essentially, he offered no results at all. Instead, there were bare texts, and the suggestions they

Der Beruf des Schneiders stirbt aus.

Der Beruf des Schneiders stirbt aus. Er war der Kommissionär des gesellschaftlichen Verkehrs. Er vermittelte den Individualanspruch mit dem gesellschaftlichen. Die vorbürgerliche Welt war standesgemäß uniformiert, erst der freie Bürger brauchte die Nahtstelle des Kleides, das die Intimsphäre des Körpers herausarbeitete und die Person doch zugleich gesellschaftsfähig machte. Die spontane also unwillkürliche Willkür des anything goes, das die gleichgültige Häßlichkeit der politischen Elite ebenso erlaubt wie das Markenartikelbewußtsein der Kreativen, macht den Schneider überflüssig.

Die Person als Atom und gleichzeitig beständiger Kontrahent des Gesellschaftlichen ist ein überlebtes Modell. Es scheitert am Sieg der Massenkultur. Aufmerksam zu machen gilt es aber auf den Zusammenhang, der zwischen dem fatalen Kult des nackten oder in wallende Laken gehüllten Adepten der Lebensreform und den ausgefeilten Interieurs des Jugendstils besteht. Je weniger nämlich das Kleid dem Einzelnen Halt zu geben vermag, desto wichtiger werden Interieurs, Dispositionen im Raum, die als zweite Haut getragen werden können. Der auf kommunikative Settings Angewiesene definiert sich nicht länger als Einzelner, im Gegenteil: er erfährt sich gerade als Connaisseur von möglicherweise sehr unterschiedlichen kommunikativen Situationen, an denen er zu partizipieren versteht. Das Ambiente ist sein Ich, das Design seine Eigenschaft.

Alfredo Arribas ist der Maßschneider solcher Ambienti. Ich hatte das wirkliche Vergnügen, einer solchen Investitur beizuwohnen. Im Rahmen von Design Horizonte 1990 stellte Alfredo Arribas erstmals Arbeiten in Frankfurt vor. Sie wurden in der Rotunde der Schirn Kunsthalle präsentiert. Die Stühle, Armstühle und Sitzbänke »Jane Greystoke« die man bewundern konnte, wirkten auf dem Boden der Betontonne, wo sie plaziert waren, durchaus fehl am Platze. Hervorragende handwerkliche Verarbeitung von Holz, Stahl und Leder vermittelte indessen dem Sitzenden das Gefühl, völlig akzeptiert zu sein.

Das Schirn Café befand sich damals in einem beklagenswerten Zustand. Von Café konnte überhaupt nicht die Rede sein. Dafür waren die das Lokal Betreibenden der Grund. Man darf aber ebenso sagen, daß ein unmöglicher Raum die adäquaten Betreiber gefunden hatte. Trotzdem war es weniger innere Überzeugung als ein ausgeprägter Respekt vor den Lieblingsspielzeugen seiner Mitarbeiter, die Christoph Vitali, den Herren der Schirn, schließlich dem Plan zustimmen ließen, Alfredo Arribas zu einer Ideenskizze für eine Umgestaltung des Schirn Cafés aufzufordern.

Für Arribas war Frankfurt damals noch eine terra incognita. Meine Befürchtung, er könnte mit einem fertigen Design-Konzept aufwarten, das dann dauerhaft so fehl am Platze wirken würde wie seine zweifellos schönen Stühle in der Rotunde, war nicht nur unbegründet, es trat das genaue Gegenteil ein. Es gab so gut wie gar keine Ergebnisse. Statt dessen gab es karge Texte, deren Man-könnte-Prosa deutlich machte, daß sie eher Fragen als Vorschläge enthielten, sowie eine unersättliche Neugier auf alles, was es in Frankfurt an gastronomischem Bestand kennenzulernen lohne. Daß man ihm wenig zeigen konnte, frustrierte ihn nicht, sondern schien nur sein Interesse zu wecken. Im übrigen zog er mit der Kamera durch die Stadt und machte zahllose Aufnahmen von Fassaden, Plätzen und Architekturdetails. Als Ergebnis des Auftrages konnten weder Grundrisse, noch Schnitte, geschweige denn Details einer konstruktiven Umsetzung präsentiert werden.

Erst nach und nach wurde mir klar, daß die Aufgabe, die wir Alfredo Arribas gestellt hatten, für ihn ebenso unmöglich zu erfüllen war, wie es für einen verantwortungsvollen Schneider unmöglich gewesen wäre, einen Gentleman einzukleiden, den er noch nie gesehen hatte. Er war schlicht zu klug, um sich der Illusion hinzugeben, er könne uns einen Entwurf für etwas liefern, von dem wir selbst keine Idee hatten.

Was schließlich als das neue Schirn Café entstand, war der langwierige Prozeß, einem Skelett zunächst einen Körper zu verschaffen, den es dann einzukleiden galt. Dieser Körper ist nun aber nicht etwas, was zwischen Skelett und Kleidung zu denken ist. Vielmehr ist es die Genialität eines Ambiente-Schneiders, wie Alfredo Arribas einer ist, die imaginierte kommunikative Situation - denn diese ist der Körper eines Raumes - so exakt vorauszudenken, daß die vorweg zu entwerfende Kleidung exakt sitzt. Unendliche Sorgfalt legt Alfredo Arribas deshalb auf Fragen wie die, wer wen in welcher Situation sehen soll, wo was von wem zu hören ist, welches Licht wann im Laufe eines Tages zu welcher Speisekarte paßt. Die Antworten auf solche Fragen - und tausend verwandte - definieren den Körper, den es im Planungsprozeß antizipatorisch zu fassen gilt. Nur wenn dies gelingt, wird der kollektive Körper, als den man sich die kommunizierenden Besucher des Schirn Cafés vorstellen muß, so bequem sitzen wie der Einzelne auf dem Greystoke-Sessel und dabei in seinem Gefühl des Angenommenseins so unbeeindruckt bleiben von den unmöglichen Gebäuden (etwa dem Technischen Rathaus), des Umfeldes wie der auf dem Greystoke-Sessel Sitzende gegenüber dem Deplacement dieses Möbels in der Rotunde der Schirn Kunsthalle. Oft sind die Design-Szene im allgemeinen und Alfredo Arribas im besonderen als outrierte Selbstdarsteller und -verwirklicher charakterisiert worden. Über die Design-Szene habe ich nicht zu sprechen; Alfredo Arribas aber habe ich als den exakten Gegenpol dieses Typus kennengelernt und ich bin sicher, daß gerade darin seine eigentliche Bedeutung liegt. Für die Ambienti Alfredo Arribas', die einem Kollektiv für die paar Stunden seines Zusammenseins das Gefühl der Adäquatheit vermitteln, gilt, was auch für die Garderobe eines wirklich gut angezogenen Gentleman charakteristisch war: sie hatte so gut zu sitzen, daß ihre Vorzüglichkeit gar nicht mehr auffiel.

contained along the lines of »one could ...« entailed questions rather than proposals, as well as an insatiable curiosity regarding every gastronomic detail of Frankfurt that might be worth investigating. The fact that there was little to show did not frustrate him, and instead seemed merely to whet his appetite. Otherwise, he went about town with his camera, taking countless pictures of facades, squares and architectural details. This assignment yielded no results, neither layouts nor sectional drawings, let alone the details of how to translate these into constructive building work.

Only gradually did it become clear to me that the task we had asked Alfredo Arribas to fulfil was as impossible for him to perform as if it would have been for a responsible tailor to clothe a gentlemen whom he had never before set eyes on. He was simply too intelligent to be fooled by the illusion that he could provide us with a design for something of which we ourselves had no idea.

What finally emerged as the new Schirn Café was the result of a lengthy process of first providing the skeleton with a body, and then clothing the body. However, this body is not merely to be thought of as coming between the skeleton and the clothing. Rather, it is the genius of an ambiance tailor, and Alfredo Arribas is indeed such a tailor, who can plan out imagined communicative situations (the body of a space) with such precision that the clothing to be designed ahead of time ends up fitting perfectly. This is why Alfredo Arribas pays the utmost attention to questions such as who is to be seen by whom in which situation, what is to be heard from whom and where, what kind of light goes with which menu at which time of day. The answers to such questions, as well as thousands of other related issues, define the body which must be conceived during the planning process in anticipation of what is to come later. Only if this succeeds will the collective body – and we must conceive of the communicating guests at the Schirn Café as precisely such a body – sit as comfortably as the individual on the Greystoke armchair, and in doing so be so immersed in a feeling of acceptance that it remains untouched by impossible buildings nearby like the Technical City Hall, just as the person sitting in the Greystoke armchair is oblivious to how out of place such furniture is in the Schirn Kunsthalle rotunda.

The design scene in general, and Alfredo Arribas in particular, are often portrayed as being exaggerated posers and self-realizers. It is not my task here to discuss the design world. However, my experience with Alfredo Arribas is that he is the diametrical opposite of this characterization. I am also certain that this is exactly wherein his true importance lies. His ambiances, which provide a collective body with a sense of adequate surroundings for a few hours, are guided by the same principle as the clothes of a truly well-dressed gentleman: they must fit so well that their excellence is no longer conspicuous.

Building...   Bauend...

Enric Miralles

... while there are architects who still believe the city is a place where one builds small garden temples to honor some ruler or other...
Oh, or even worse: his boulevards!
    And the others find their city by crossing a highway with a supermarket...
Alfredo seems to play architecture like a game.
    His drawings are like little riddles:
    Yellow on the inside,
        white on the outside.
            What is it?
Put another way, not like a game, but like a gymnastics exercise. Alfredo is getting into shape.
    These projects are a kind of training.
His constructions have been transformed into something very elastic in places where everything one can imagine might just happen...

        • • •

This training, this observing-oneself-in-the-mirror, this trying out movements and figures – this is architectonic, it clearly belongs to the purpose and the guild of architecture.
    In these projects – and I don't think Alfredo would disagree – the typological root, perhaps even the assessment, is that the practice of architecture, its pursuit, refers to architecture itself...
        Here, notes and sections appear...
      enabling Arribas to engage in a dialogue with architects and projects which he admires, and which always remain visible in his work.
    He never conceals his admiration for the works of others, such as Carlo Mollinos, Toyo Itos, etc... This admiration is transformed into practice, into exercise, even during the initial drawings...

This is the most personal moment in his work.

    While at the same time the concept of these projects always remains collective.

.. während es Architekten gibt, die noch immer glauben, die Stadt sei ein Ort, wo man Gartentempelchen für irgendeinen Herrscher baut ...
Oh, oder noch schlimmer: seine Prachtstraßen!
    Und die anderen finden ihre Stadt in der Kreuzung einer Autobahn und eines Supermarktes ...
Alfredo scheint die Architektur wie ein Spiel zu betreiben.
    Seine Zeichnungen sind wie kleine Rätsel:
        Innen gelb, außen weiß.
            Was ist das?
Besser gesagt, nicht wie ein Spiel, sondern wie eine Gymnastikübung, Alfredo macht sich fit.
    Diese Projekte sind ein Training.
Seine Bauten haben sich in etwas sehr Dehnbares verwandelt, in Orte, wo all das, was man sich vorstellen mag, möglicherweise passiert ...

        • • •

Dieses Training, dieses Sich-selbst-vor-dem-Spiegel-Beobachten, dieses Ausprobieren von Bewegungen und Figuren, das ist architektonisch, das gehört eindeutig zum Sinn und zur Zunft der Architektur:
    In diesen Projekten – und ich glaube nicht, daß Alfredo mir da widersprechen würde –, gibt es eine typologische Wurzel, ja sogar die Einschätzung, die Praxis der Architektur, ihre Ausübung, beziehe sich auf sie selbst ...
        Hier tauchen Notizen, Schnitte auf ..,
    die es ihm erlauben, mit Architekten und Projekten, die Arribas bewundert und die stets in seinem Werk sichtbar bleiben, in einen Dialog zu treten.
    Seine Bewunderung für die Arbeiten anderer, wie Carlo Mollino, Toyo Ito, etc. ... wird niemals versteckt.
Jene Bewunderung formt sich bereits in den ersten Skizzen in Praxis, in Übung um ...

    Das ist der persönlichste Moment seiner Arbeit.

    Währenddessen die Vorstellung von diesen Projekten stets eine kollektive bleibt.

Diese im Entstehen befindlichen Räume reißen jeden, der sich den Ort vorstellt und innerlich erschafft, genauso mit wie den Architekten.
    In diesem Moment entweicht seine Architektur der Übung,
                            dem Training:
es sind Würfel, die über einen Spieltisch geworfen werden.
Alfredo Arribas erscheint als Croupier und das Spiel -das Projekt- liegt in den Händen und Hoffnungen der aufmerksamen Spieler am Tisch ...
    Alfredo muß weiter die Würfel werfen, damit das Spiel am
    Laufen bleibt.
        Diesen Prozess aufrechtzuerhalten ist die schwierige
        Schwebe, in der sich das Werk von Arribas hält.
Während man unbeweglich, lächelnd dasteht, mag es schwierig sein, zu unterscheiden, wer sich setzt, um am Spieltisch mitzuspielen und wer ein Falschspieler ist, der gezinkte Karten im Ärmel hat ...
    Aber es scheint, als ob Alfredo diejenigen erkennt,
                            die Fallen stellen ...

Die Auftraggeber, die darum gebeten haben mitzuspielen, scheinen das Spiel zu genießen,
        ...wie er die Karten flink und geschickt austeilt ...
    ...wie die unterschiedlichen Blätter
        auf dem Tisch entstehen und vergehen ...
...die schwindelerregende Abfolge von sich wiederholenden Bewegungen ... so schnell, so diszipliniert ...

Es ist wichtig, daß seine Figur dort weiterhin
die Karten auf dem Tisch verteilt.
        Ich weiß nicht, wie er es macht ..,
            aber ich bin sicher, er macht vieles.

These spaces in the process of emerging sweep away everyone who imagines and creates them from within, just as the architect himself is swept off his feet by them.
    At this moment, his architecture gives
                exercise, training, the slip.
    Dice are being rolled onto a card table.
Alfredo Arribas appears as the croupier and the game - the project - is in the hands and hopes of the attentive players at the table...
    Alfredo has to keep rolling the dice
    so that the game may continue.
        Keeping up this process is the delicate
        state of suspension of Arribas' work.
While one stands there immobile, smiling, it may be difficult to distinguish who is sitting down at the card table in order to play, and who is a cheater, with marked cards up his sleeve...
    But it seems that Alfredo knows
        which of them is setting traps...

The clients, who have asked to play, seem to be enjoying the game,
        ... as he shuffles the cards
        and deals them skillfully...
    ...as the different hands appear
    and disappear from the table...
... the dizzying sequence of movements that repeat themselves... so quickly, so disciplined...

It is important that his figure continue to deal the cards onto the table.
        I don't know how he does it...
        but I am certain
        that he does quite a lot.

Excessive velocity as the norm

Überhöhte Geschwindigkeit als Normalzustand

Georg-Christof Bertsch

For quite a long time, Alfredo Arribas (born in 1954 in Barcelona) was treated as an exotic by the apologists of »great architecture«, and not really taken seriously. Instead, his work became the crystallization point of a vehement debate in lectures, newspapers and design journals (at first in Barcelona, after 1989 on an international level as well) as to whether »leisure time architecture« was even worth speaking about as a subject of consequence. The rapid development of the genre soon rendered this discussion superfluous. Oscar Tusquets, who in 1986 was still quite alone with his plea that bar architecture be taken seriously, was not so long afterward acclaimed as one of the initiators of this approach. For the great architects of the older generation, bar design was never anything more than a tiresome stage between one's studies and »true architecture«, a stage that designers gladly hid in their back closets as soon as »real projects« could be undertaken.

Arribas recognized the essential role and the (figuratively speaking) very definite »urban planning« function of central nightlife locales. Parallel to purebred designers such as Philippe Starck or interior designers like Dani Freixes, Arribas turned bar design into a high art form. This made him the subject of both envy and scorn. One thing about him was particularly annoying: Alfredo Arribas never gave his critics and opponents enough time to compose detailed indictments against him; he was simply too productive. His knowledge, his quick wit and eloquence, and even his charm were simply proverbial. His steadily growing body of work in itself made him convincing - not only quantitatively speaking, but also immeasurably in terms of structure and system. Patterns emerged, not least of all his brilliant treatment of the genius loci, as it has been mastered by only very few architects.

Critics prophesied that Arribas would soon become passé, even as it became apparent that his earlier projects »Velvet Bar« (1987) or the discotheque »Louis Vega« were sensational commercial successes for the respective clients. Not only were the projects larger, they were also increasingly originating from outside Spain: from Italy, Japan, and Germany, for example. Whereupon critics predicted that Arribas' studio would fold after the Olympics boom at the very latest (Barcelona hosted the 1992 Olympics), as it had only been carried along by the wave of this hubris. In fact, the exact opposite occurred - the wave of bankruptcies sweeping through the studios in Barcelona did not come anywhere close to affecting Arribas. Finally, the word was that Arribas was only capable of "small", if spectacular, interior renovations.

Alfredo Arribas (*1954 in Barcelona) wurde lange Zeit von den Apologeten der »großen Architektur« als Exot behandelt und nicht wirklich ernst genommen. Stattdessen wurde sein Werk zum Kristallisationspunkt einer heftigen Debatte in Vorträgen, Tageszeitungen und Designzeitschriften (zunächst innerhalb Barcelonas, ab 1989 auch international), ob »Freizeitarchitektur« es überhaupt Wert sei, ernsthaft besprochen zu werden. Die rasche Entwicklung des Genres machte diese Diskussion bald überflüssig. Oscar Tusquets, der mit seinem Plädoyer für die Ernsthaftigkeit von Bararchitektur 1986 noch allein auf weiter Flur stand, wurde bald als einer der Initiatoren dieser Sichtweise gefeiert. Für die großen Architekten der älteren Generation war Bargestaltung stets nur ein leidiger Schritt zwischen Studium und »eigentlicher Architektur« gewesen, ein Schritt, den man später gerne versteckte, sobald man »richtige« Projekte realisieren konnte.

Arribas erkannte die essentielle Bedeutung und die (im übertragenen Sinne) geradezu »städtebauliche« Funktion von zentralen Orten der Nacht. Er entwickelte, parallel zu Vollblut-Designern wie Philippe Starck oder Interiordesignern wie Dani Freixes die Bargestaltung zu einer großen Kunst. Darum beneidete, darum verachtete man ihn. Besonders eines hat man ihm verübelt: Alfredo Arribas hat seinen Kritikern und Gegnern nie die Zeit gelassen, ausführliche Anklageschriften zu verfassen, seine Produktivität war zu groß, sein Wissen, seine Schlagfertigkeit und Eloquenz, schließlich sein Charme geradezu sprichwörtlich. Er konnte schon allein durch sein stetig wachsendes Werk überzeugen - nicht nur quantitativ, sondern in einem schließlich unübersehbaren Maße auch strukturell und systematisch. Muster wurden sichtbar, zu denen nicht zuletzt der souveräne Umgang mit dem genius loci gehört, wie er von nur wenigen Architekten beherrscht wird.

Die Kritiker prophezeiten Arribas einen baldigen Absturz, selbst dann noch, als es sich abzeichnete, daß sich seine frühen Aufträge, Velvet Bar (1987) oder die Diskothek Louie Vega, zu kommerziellen Sensationserfolgen für die Auftraggeber entwickelten. Die Aufträge wurden jedoch nicht nur größer, sie kamen zusehends mehr aus dem Ausland: Italien, Japan, Deutschland. Die Kritiker prophezeiten daraufhin, daß das Studio Arribas spätestens nach dem Olympia-Boom (Barcelona war 1992 Olympiastadt), untergehen würde, denn es sei nur durch diese Hybris nach oben gespült worden. Das Gegenteil war der Fall - die Pleitewelle unter den Studios in Barcelona schwappte weit an Arribas vorbei. Man munkelte schließlich, Arribas sei nur in der Lage, »kleine«, wenn auch spektakuläre, Umbauten zu realisieren. Auch hier sollte das Gegenteil der Fall sein. Marugame in Fukuoka (Japan) und der sehr große Gebäudekomplex Hung Kuo in Shanghai (China) belegen dies.

Heute kann man sagen, daß das Studio eine Plattform erreicht hat, die nicht mehr substantiell angegriffen wird. Arribas wird als bedeutender internationaler Architekt akzeptiert.

Der Umfang der Aufträge offenbarte zugleich immer mehr die architektonische Kapazität dieses Studios. Doch was heißt »architektonische Kapazität« außer rein quantitativer Leistung?

In der Baubranche unterscheidet man gerne zwischen den sogenannten »Entwurfsarchitekten« (Frank Gehry soll solch einer sein) und den »Ausführungsarchitekten«, die Pläne umsetzen und dabei nicht viel nachdenken. In den USA hat sich diese duale, ja nachgerade polare Sichtweise weitgehend durchgesetzt. Das »Genie« entwirft, der »Ingenieur« setzt um. Diese Betrachtung widerspricht in jeder Hinsicht der Idee vom Gesamtkunstwerk, die Joseph Maria Olbrich (1867-1908), Antoní Gaudí (1852-1926) oder Gunnar Asplund (1885-1940) vertraten. Genau diesen Architekten jedoch fühlt sich Arribas verpflichtet. Und gerade deshalb befaßt er sich nicht nur mit dem groben Entwurf, sondern auch mit der Detaildurchführung. Er stellt seine Entwürfe in einen kulturellen Kontext. Er integriert dabei die Schöpfungen anderer, gleichberechtigter Künstler. Nicht umsonst findet man bei den Baudokumentationen stets die Namen der Grafikdesigner, mit denen er kooperiert hat, Sonsoles Llorens, Pati Nuñez, Alfonso Sostres, Capella/Larrea, Xavier Mariscal, ... ja, in manchen Fällen spielen sogar die Modedesigner - die für Bartender und Personal Entwürfe geschaffen haben - eine Rolle. Namen wie Chu Uroz, der Chefdesigner des spanischen Modeherstellers Armand Basi, stehen hierfür.

Auch die Musik für einen Ort, wie die Groß-Bar Torres de Avila (1990) wurde speziell designt; Mingus Formenter, einer der ersten Namen unter spanischen DJs zeichnet hierfür verantwortlich.

Arribas ist ein anerkannt guter Entwurfszeichner. Er befaßt sich lange analytisch mit den Gegebenheiten und kontextbezogenen Charakteristika eines Ortes, bevor er eine erste Zeichnung anfertigt. Diese jedoch erinnert an japanische Tuschmalereien des Suiboko aus dem 15. Jahrhundert: schnell und präzise, jedoch offen für Interpretationen. Arribas' künstlerischen Zeichnungen, mit grobem Stift ausgeführt, werden an den Raumgegebenheiten abgeschliffen, direkter auf sie bezogen, Ansichten, Atmosphären entstehen, die sich langsam in Planungszeichnungen transformieren.

An dieser Stelle setzt die sprichwörtliche Präzision des Studios unter Arribas' Partner, Miguel Morte, ein. Entwürfe entwickeln sich in atemberaubender Geschwindigkeit zu Plänen 1:100, 1:50, 1:25. Aber selbst hier hören sie nicht auf. Für Barna Crossing (Fukuoka, Japan, 1989) wurden

Here as well, fact ran contrary to expectation, as evidenced by »Marugame« in Fukuoka (Japan) and the enormous »Hung Kuo« building complex in Shanghai (China).

Today, the studio can be said to have reached a level where it is no longer attacked. Arribas is accepted as a major international architect. The expanding scope of his projects also attests to the architectural capacity of the studio. But what is »architectural capacity« beyond purely quantitative performance?

In the construction sector, people like to distinguish between the so-called »blueprint architects« (Frank Gehry is supposedly one of these) and »realization architects«, who simply implement plans without giving them much thought. In the U.S., this dual, or even polar, way of looking at things has been largely accepted. The »genius« creates the designs, and the »engineer« carries them out. Such an attitude is completely at odds with the concept of the Gesamtkunstwerk put forward by Joseph Maria Olbrich (1867-1908), Antoní Gaudí (1852-1926) or Gunnar Asplund (1885-1940). However, it is precisely to these architects that Arribas feels indebted. And this is also why he is concerned not only with the rough design, but also with how the details are implemented. One could say he places his designs in a cultural context, while integrating the creations of other artists who are on an equal footing with himself. It is no coincidence that the documentations of his buildings invariably include the names of the graphic designers who cooperated with him on the project: Sonsoles Llorens, Pati Nuñez, Alfonso Sostres, Capella/Larrea, Xavier Mariscal... in fact, in some cases even the fashion designers who have created designs for bartenders and staff are included in the credits. Names such as Chu Uroz, head designer of the Spanish garment producer Armand Basi, are examples of this.

Even the music has been specially designed for a locale such as the large »Torres de Avila« club. Mingus Formenter, one of the top names among Spanish DJs, is in charge of this task.

Arribas' skill at draftsmanship is widely recognized. He spends a great deal of time analyzing the circumstances and context-related characteristics of a place before making a first draft, but the draft itself is reminiscent of Japanese Suiboko watercolors from the 15th century - quick and precise, yet open for interpretation. Arribas' artis-tic drawings, done in coarse pencil, are honed down to fit the spatial circumstances, related to them more directly. Perspectives and atmospheres emerge which are slowly transformed into plans.

This is where the proverbial precision of the studio comes into play under the direction of Arribas' partner Miguel Morte. Designs develop into plans at breathtaking speed on a scale of 1:100, 1:50, 1:25. But they do not stop here. For »Barna Crossing« (Fukuoka, Japan, 1989), detail drawings down to a scale of 1:1 were made in order to portray the mountings and specially designed screws.

Arribas is just as concise in this respect as he is when developing the concept for the ground plan. His design work thus cannot be considered separately from his architectural work. Alessandro Mendini (in »Architect Designers of the Eighties«, Barcelona 1987, p.7) has commented that »there are architects who are also active as designers«. However, this does not apply to Arribas. He is not an architect-designer, like Norman Foster, for example (born in 1936), who created a typical architectural design with his famous Nomos table system. Nor is he a designer-architect like Matteo Thun (born in 1952), who always manages to simply miniaturize architectonic construction principles by »scale jumping«. Arribas is also not a pop-art architect like Frank Gehry, who would monumentalize a telescope when designing a new building for the advertising agency »Chiat Day« (San Francisco, 1993), as a symbol of the creative world view of the client.

Arribas embodies a much more straightforward, and at the same time historically older, position: he takes a Renaissance approach. He seeks the internal logic which holds together the various standards and utilization contexts for the sum of all artistic details, yet without applying a stiff, formal grid. Thus, his rooms cannot be »furnished«, since they are integral in design from the very beginning. All details which ultimately form a part of them are components of the original planning process. This is what creates the strong impression of the »artist's hand« that one senses in his projects. And this is also why, in the case of Arribas, »creation« ought to replace the terms »design« and »architecture«, still at odds with one another, and reconcile them. As an architect who is equipped with all the trappings of architecture, Arribas has consciously opened up a field of application, a functional area within architecture that is a dangerous can of worms: designing interiors for bars and restaurants. This is an area in which - as in hardly any other - the result determines whether the client will survive or go under, often within a matter of weeks. After all, the location is supposed to create a sense of well-being, and no one, but no one, can be forced to go to a bar, a restaurant or a disco - which makes for a situation quite different from that of hospitals, schools, public buildings, airports - in a word, places for great architecture.

This fact was first understood by »la gente guapa«, the jet-set of Barcelona, who only enjoy a gin and tonic when it is served in an appropriate atmosphere. It also made a difference who had created the right ambiance, for a trend began to emerge in the Eighties which has continued unabated up to the present day: nothing is more unattractive than anonymity and namelessness.

Detailzeichnungen bis 1:1 angefertigt, um die Aufhängungen und speziell entworfene Schrauben darstellen zu können. An dieser Stelle ist Arribas genauso konzis wie in der Entwicklung der Grundrißidee. Sein Designwerk läßt sich daher nicht von seinem architektonischen Werk trennen. Die Feststellung Alessandro Mendinis (in »Architekten Designer der 80er Jahre«, Barcelona 1987, S. 7): »Es gibt Architekten, die ebenso als Designer tätig sind« trifft für Arribas insofern nicht zu. Er ist auch kein Architekten-Designer, wie etwa Norman Foster (*1936), der mit dem berühmten Tischsystem Nomos ein typisches Architektendesign geschaffen hat, oder ein Designer-Architekt, wie Matteo Thun (*1952), dem es immer wieder gelingt, im »scale jumping« architektonische Konstruktionsprinzipien schlicht zu miniaturisieren. Arribas ist auch kein Popart-Architekt, wie Frank Gehry, der beim Neubau der Werbeagentur »Chiat Day« (San Francisco, 1993) ein Fernglas monumentalisierte (als Symbol des kreativen Weitblicks des Auftaggebers).

Arribas verkörpert eine viel schlichtere und zugleich historisch ältere Position: er verfolgt eine Renaissance-Haltung. Er sucht die innere Logik, welche die unterschiedlichen Maßstäbe und Nutzungszusammenhänge der Summe aller gestalterischen Details zusammenhält, jedoch, ohne ein starres formales Raster anzulegen. Man kann seine Räume von daher nicht »möblieren«, da sie von vornherein integral gedacht sind. Alle Details, die sie schließlich bevölkern, sind Bestandteil der ursprünglichen Planung. Dies macht das starke Gefühl der gestalterischen Handschrift aus, welche man in seinen Projekten stets empfindet. »Gestaltung« sollte daher bei ihm auch die noch immer feindlichen Begriffe »Design« und »Architektur« ersetzen und sie versöhnen. Arribas hat sich bewußt - als Architekt und mit der gesamten Klaviatur der Architektur ausgestattet - ein Anwendungsfeld, ein Funktionsfeld von Architektur eröffnet, das eine riskante Schlangengrube ist: Gestaltung von gastronomischen Räumen. Dies ist ein Feld, in dem - wie kaum sonst - das Resultat über Triumph oder Konkurs des Auftraggebers entscheidet, oft binnen weniger Wochen. Denn der Ort soll Wohlbefinden schaffen - und niemand, wirklich niemand ist gezwungen, eine Bar, ein Restaurant, eine Diskothek zu besuchen - ganz im Gegensatz zu Krankenhäusern, Schulen, öffentlichen Gebäuden, Flughäfen, also Orten der »großen Architektur«.

Zuerst begriff das »la gente guapa«, die jeunesse dorée Barcelonas, denen der Gin Tonic nur schmeckt, wenn er in einem angesagten Ambiente serviert wird. Auch wer solch ein Ambiente gestaltete war enorm wichtig, denn in den 80er Jahren begann ein bis heute unaufhaltsamer Trend deutlich zu werden: nichts ist unattraktiver als Anonymität und Namenlosigkeit. Das begann sich auch auf Innenarchitekturen, Design und Architektur auszuwirken. Gegen diese Anonymität und Neutralität, die so charakteristisch für viele Räume der Klassischen Moderne war, standen die programmatisch individuellen Ausprägungen der gestalterischen Lösungen von Arribas. Gegen die Anonymität stand aber auch die Person Arribas und die Gruppe von Spitzengestaltern sämtlicher Genres, die als Personen das Projekt mittrugen. Wo diese Individualität ihre stärksten Ausformungen erlebte, da war das Gefühl des Angemessenen, des Coolen, Akzeptablen am größten. Gerade das ist meines Erachtens in den Räumen von Alfredo Arribas am ausgeprägtesten auf der ganzen Welt.

Die Suche nach Individualität und Charakterstärke von Orten hat sich mit der noch immer ungebrochenen Zerstörung der Innenstädte und deren Entvölkerung nur noch verstärkt. Das Bedürfnis nach individuellen Orten, nach halböffentlicher Privatheit und nach dem Ort als »zweitem Kleid« hat sich zugespitzt. Sich schmücken können mit einem Gebäude, diese in der Renaissance und bis zu Beginn des 20. Jahrhunderts so selbstverständliche Grundanforderung des Auftraggebers, dieser Aufgabe kommt Alfredo Arribas mit der größten Selbstverständlichkeit nach, weil er sich selbst mit den Projekten schmücken will. Und deshalb steht er auch zu allen seinen Lösungen, bis in die Details.

In dem Band »Alfredo Arribas Architecture & Design 1986-1992«, erschienen 1993 im gleichen Verlag, konnte ich die Arbeiten der »Barepoche«, wie ich sie heute nennen möchte, ausführlich darstellen. Aber erst in diesem Band mit den Werken 1993-96 kommen die größeren, teils sehr umfangreichen Projekte zum Tragen, mit denen Alfredo Arribas Arquitectos Asociados in jüngster Zeit beauftragt wurde. Die gestalterische Sprache wird konzentrierter, großzügiger, es ist spürbar, daß mit den größeren Flächen ein regelrechtes Durchatmen einhergeht, welches jedoch mit einer bemerkenswerten Disziplin geschieht. Arribas steht an der Schwelle zu einem großen internationalen Büro ohne die unmittelbare Nutzerbezogenheit aus dem Auge zu verlieren, Nutzerbezogenheit im Sinne des Auftraggebers, des einzelnen Menschen, der die Räume benutzt aber auch in bezug auf sich selbst. Den Charme seiner ersten kleinen Barprojekte versteht er in anderen Dimensionen, in anderen Aufgaben immer wieder aufs neue auferstehen zu lassen. Er gehört ganz offensichtlich nicht zu jenen, die frühe Projekte verleugnen, um sich auf die »eigentliche« Architektur zu konzentrieren. Es wird vielmehr umgekehrt deutlich, wieviel schon in den frühesten Interior-Projekten angelegt war. Eine Revision der frühen Arbeiten zeigt die langangelegte Strategie. Erstaunlich genug in einer so schnellebigen Epoche und bei der überhöhten Geschwindigkeit, mit der sich Arribas in ihr bewegt.

This then carried over to interior decor, design, and architecture. The anonymity and neutrality so characteristic of many spaces shaped by Classical Modernism were countered by the programmatically individual features of Arribas' artistic solutions. However, Arribas as an individual, as well as the group of top designers from all genres who, as individuals, supported the project, were also opposed to anonymity. Where this individuality took on its most intense shape, the feeling of appropriateness, coolness, acceptability was the strongest. In my opinion, it is precisely this feeling that is more pronounced in spaces designed by Alfredo Arribas than anywhere else in the entire world.

The search for individuality and strength of character in places has only become stronger with the ongoing destruction and depopulation of the inner cities. The need for individual places, for semi-public privacy and a place that functions as a kind of »second clothing« has become more urgent. Being able to adorn oneself with a building, a basic demand on the part of the client which, in the Renaissance and up until the 20th century, was so self-evident - it is this task which Alfredo Arribas pursues as the most self-evident truth, for he wants to adorn himself with the projects. And this is also why he stands by all of his solutions, down to the details.

In the volume »Alfredo Arribas Architecture & Design 1986-1992«, published by the same company in 1993, I had an opportunity to provide a detailed presentation of the works of the »bar epoch«, as I would like to refer to it today. However, the larger, in some cases extremely comprehensive projects with which Alfredo Arribas' Arquitectos Asociados have recently been commissioned only come to bear in this new volume, which contains the works from 1993 to 1996. The creative idiom is becoming more concentrated, more liberal. The larger surfaces bring with them a breath of fresh air, yet are executed with remarkable discipline. Arribas is on the verge of joining the ranks of major international studios, yet without losing sight of the immediate relationship to the user - which is to say not only to the client, the individual who uses the rooms as such, but also in relation to himself. He understands how to resurrect the charm of his first small bar projects in other dimensions, in other new tasks. Quite obviously, he is not one of those who shrug off their early projects in order to concentrate on »true architecture«. Rather, quite the opposite becomes clear - just how much was already present in his earliest interior design projects. An examination of earlier works reveals the strategy applied over a long period of time. Astonishing enough in such a fast-paced era, and at the excessive speeds at which Alfredo Arribas moves.

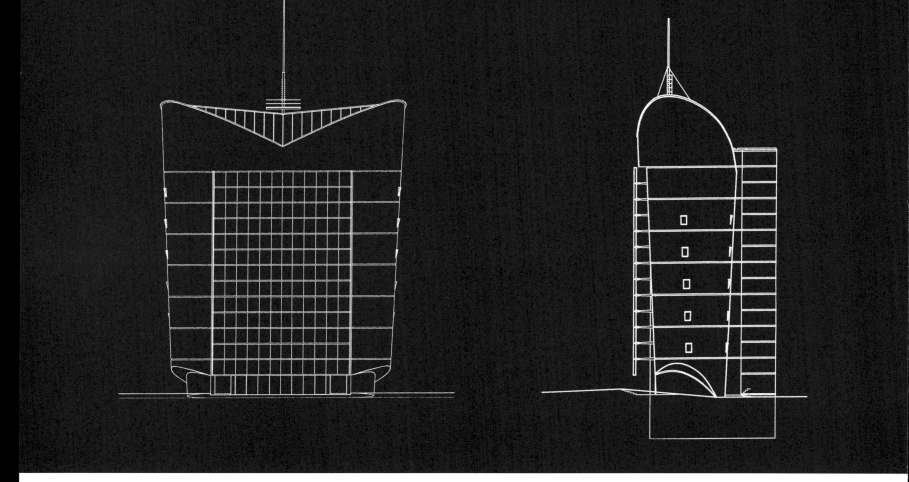

MARUGAME
Japan, 1991-93

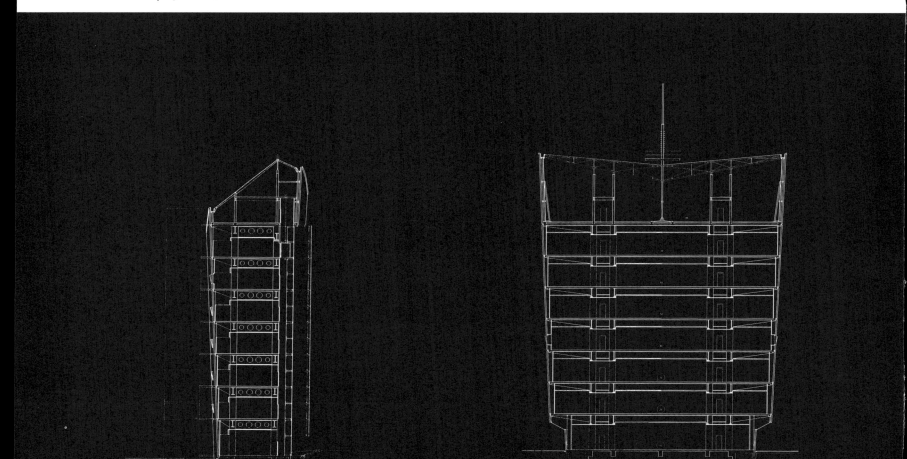

MARUGAME

Verwaltungsbau für eine Rundfunkstation und Museum für zeitgenössische spanische Kunst, Shiko-ku, Japan, 1991-93

Administration building for a network station and Museum of Contemporary Spanish Art. Japan, 1991-93

Das Gebäude wirkt in der typisch ortlosen Struktur japanischer Vorstädte wie ein ruhender Punkt, wie ein Brennpunkt und eine Landmarke. Die skulpturale Durcharbeitung, die an Henry Moore und Carlo Mollino erinnert, war für Arribas nach eigenen Worten »ein geometrisches Vergnügen«, gesteigert durch die seltene Gelegenheit, einem Stadtteil ein visuelle Identifikationsmerkmal zu schenken. Ungewöhnlich für Japan ist auch der großzügige Umgang mit dem Baugrund, der es ermöglichte, das Gebäude weit von der Straßenkreuzung zurückzunehmen und so einen halböffentlichen Platz zu gewinnen. Die allegorische Referenz zwischen der Nutzung als Verwaltungsgebäude für eine Rundfunkgesellschaft und der Form eines Kofferradios der 50er Jahre hat mehrere Ebenen. Einmal ist mit dem japanischen Retrodesign der 90er Jahre, wie etwa Water Studios, der Nierenform und ihren Hybriden ein neues Feld geöffnet worden. Dieses betrifft die Zeitgenossenschaft des Entwurfs auf japanischem Boden. Andererseits strahlt das Gebäude durch die Form etwas beruhigend Gewohntes aus. Es macht die immaterielle Dienstleistung, die in seinen Mauern erbracht wird, plastisch faßbar und somit begreifbarer.

Arribas gelingt es hier, an einem Unort, ein Referenzobjekt zu schaffen, das neben seiner eigentlichen Nutzung zugleich mehrere Funktionen erfüllt. Neben seiner verortenden Eigenschaft wirkt es nachts wie eine riesige Laterne, die ein versöhnliches Licht im Umfeld verströmt. Betrachtet man den Grundriß des Terrains, fällt die erzählerische Architektursprache noch mehr auf. Die Anlage wirkt wie der Längsschnitt durch ein Ei. Das unmittelbare Umfeld des Gebäudes wirkt wie der Dotter, indem sich das Gebäude selbst als Embryo ausmachen läßt. Die Expansion, das Wachstum ist bildhaft angelegt. Die Frage »Behältnis oder Inhalt«, die Arribas über seine erste Projektstudie stellte, beantwortet sich von selbst: beides.

Within the anonymous cityscape of Japanese suburban architecture, the building serves as a point of rest, a focus, and a landmark. Working out its sculptural finish, reminiscent of Henry Moore and Carlo Mollino, turned out to be what Arribas calls »a geometrical pleasure«. This pleasure was enhanced by the rare opportunity to present a city district with a mark of visual reference. Japanese circumstances considered, the building premises are of exceptionally generous dimensions. This allows for the building to be set back from the crossroads, thus obtaining a semi-public plaza. Shaped like a transistor radio, the structure allegorically refers to its use as a radio network's administration building. This reference is twofold. Firstly, Arribas pays hommage to the contemporary Japanese retro-design (e.g. the Water Studios), which has re-vamped the organic design of the Fifties. Secondly, the building is reassuringly habitual in appearance. It imparts a somewhat haptic quality to the immaterial services rendered inside and thus enhances their understanding. Arribas succeeds in creating a referential object in a non-place, an object fulfilling several functions aside from its main purpose. A landmark during the daytime, it glows like a giant lantern at night, its conciliantory light illuminating the neighborhood. A look at the plot's layout further reveals the design's narrative architectural imagery. The construction resembles the longitudinal section of an egg, while the building's immediate surroundings compare to a yolk, inside which the building itself can be made out as an embryo. The question whether it is »container or content«, asked by Arribas with regarde to his first project-study, is self-answering: it is both.

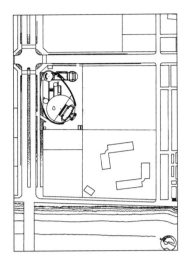

The building structures it´s faceless suburban surrounding while dominating it. Even during the construction phase it emerged as public monument and landmark.

Das Gebäude strukturiert sein gesichtsloses vorstädtisches Umfeld und dominiert es zugleich. Es hat schon während der Bauphase Wahrzeichen-Charakter bekommen und dient als Orientierungspunkt.

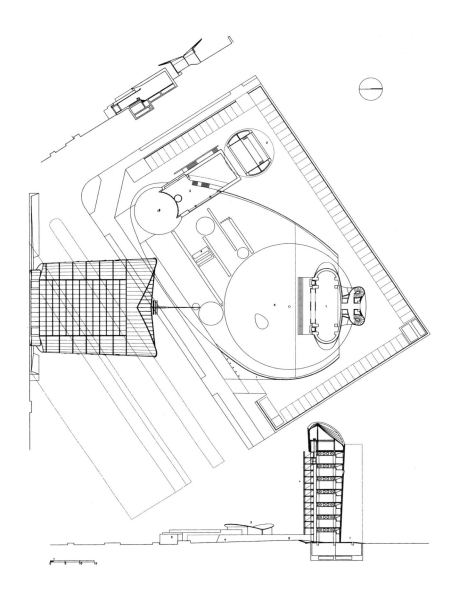

HUNG KUO BUILDING
Shanghai, China, 1994 ...

Hung Kuo Building

Business center, office and appartment compound, Shanghai, China 1994...

Geschäfts- und Bürozentrum sowie Wohnkomplex Shanghai, China, 1994...

The building stretches over an entire block set amidst three streets in a suburb of Shanghai. In order to utilize the 42000 m² of floor space for a mixture of apartments, offices, and a business center, the building had to be accessible from all sides. An underground car park had to be fitted in, with sufficient capacity to handle traffic during rush hours. Inside the building, the individual stores of the mall is arranged along a glass-roofed passageway which provides this area with daylight. Visualizing the distinction between the areas housing the mall, the cinemas, and the offices and apartments, the facade displays a classic tripartition into a high base, a transparent middle part, and an offset upper end section. Leading to the terrace in front of the cinema entrances, a grand-scale exterior staircase laid out on the longest side of this triangular building provides access to the mall level. The two towers of different size suggest a vertical tension that saves the building from a monumental appearance, and they also create a fake perspective that enhances the structure's optical depth. This latter effect compensates disadvantages of the structure's narrow layout on the triangular plot. In Hung Kuo, the sculptural style of Arribas' earlier projects is no longer plainly visible. Instead, the construction reveals a sensitive weighing and balancing of mass, vividly expressed by the two towers' varying heights.

Das Gebäude erstreckt sich über einen ganzen, von drei Straßen umgebenen, Block in der Vorstadt Shanghais. Die Mischnutzung der 42000 m² Nutzfläche als Wohnhaus, Büro- und Geschäftszentrum mit erheblichem Publikumsverkehr erforderte die Erschließung von allen Seiten sowie die Unterbringung einer geräumigen Tiefgarage, die auch in Stoßzeiten dem Autoverkehr gewachsen ist. Die Geschäfte der Mall werden im Innern durch eine mit Glas überdachte Passage erschlossen, die diesen Bereich mit natürlichem Licht versorgt. Die Differenzierung zwischen dem Bereich der Mall, der Kinos und der Büro- bzw. Wohnbereiche wird an der Fassade in einer klassischen Dreiteilung von hohem Sockel, transparentem Mittelteil und einem abgesetzten Bereich des oberen Abschlusses visualisiert. Einzelne Volumen lösen sich zaghaft aus der Sockelzone und schaffen eine gewisse geometrische Lebendigkeit. Eine großzügige Außentreppen erschließt die Ebene der Mall von der längsten Straßenseite des Dreiecks hin zur Terrasse, die den Zugang zu den drei Kinos bildet. In der Vertikalen wird durch die unterschiedliche Höhenentwicklung der beiden Türme ein Spannungsverhältnis geschaffen, das der Gesamtanlage die Monumentalität nimmt.

Zugleich wird durch die unterschiedliche Höhe der beiden Türme und die daraus resultierende falsche Perspektive eine größere optische Tiefe in den Gesamtkomplex gebracht. Damit werden Nachteile der schmalen Projektentwicklung auf dem dreieckigen Grundstück ausgeglichen. Die skulpturalen Ansätze der vorhergehenden Projekte von Arribas werden hier nur noch verhalten sichtbar. An deren Stelle tritt ein sensibles Ausgleichen und Auswägen der Volumen, was in der unterschiedlichen Höhe der beiden Türme bildhaft zum Ausdruck kommt.

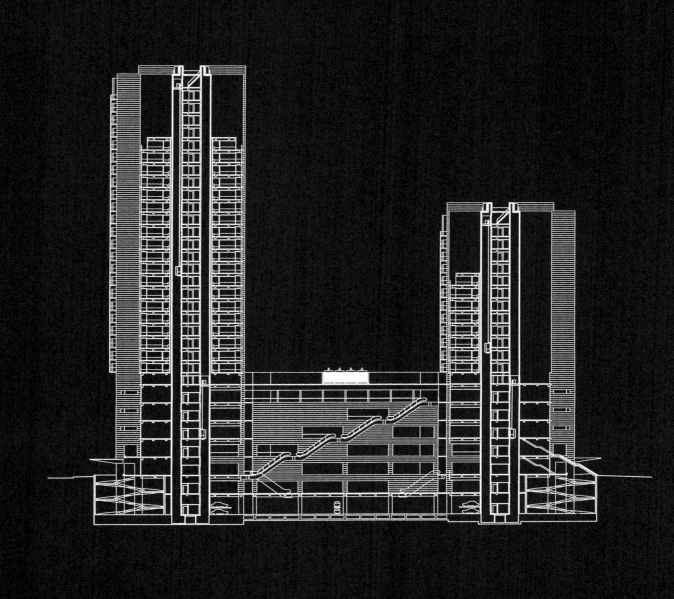

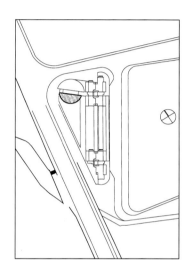

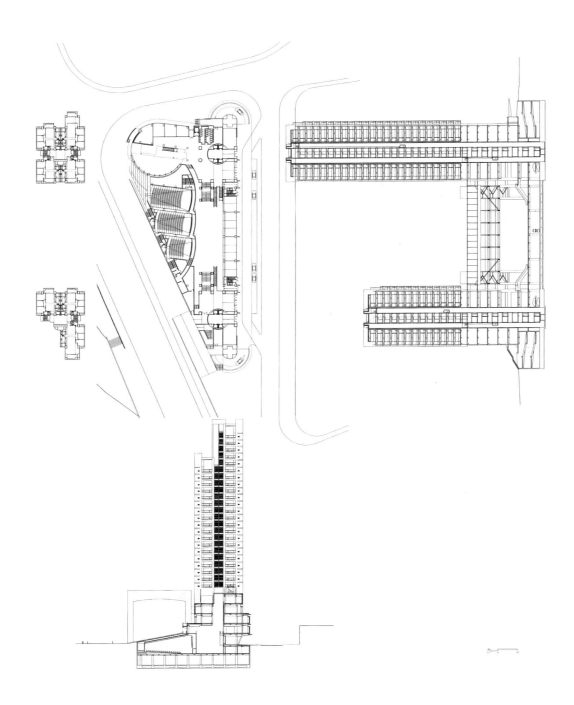

GRAN VELVET

Montigalà/Barcelona, España, 1993

GRAN VELVET

Multispace (discotheque, concert hall, bar, club) 1993, Montigalà near Barcelona

Multispace (Diskothek, Konzerthalle, Bar, Club) 1993, Montigalà bei Barcelona.

The name »Gran Velvet« refers to the bar-discotheque »Velvet« which gained Arribas a reputation as a designer and architect in 1986. Both projects were carried out for the same client, and in both cases Arribas was given an »entirely free hand«. The Gran Velvet serves as a disco for both large crowds and discerning guests. Its name boasts »Velvet« to be the generic term of a species'. The self-reference has been taken so far that a full-scale replica of the »Velvet's« center room set inside a glass cockpit hovers above the Gran Velvet's main hall. Sound-proofed against the discotheque, this cockpit houses a VIP-club and a cocktail bar. The Gran Velvet is a multispace, a type of architecture developed during the Eighties and early Nineties. It incorporates various recreational facilities and combines elements of the classic dance hall of the Forties, the discotheque of the Seventies, and the cocktail bar of the eighties. Its visitors can choose from a variety of options to indulge in - or just stroll about. This requires spacious and extensive public areas. The bars are large enough to provide guests with a quick drink even when the maximum of 5000 people crowd the place. The Gran Velvet's outside displays an industrial aesthetics which is spectacularly enhanced when the central barrel's ceiling slides open at night. As the cupola opens up, the moist, smoky air escapes from the inside and conveys the image of a cooling tower, an effect supported by scenic lighting. Representing the touristically determined economy of Catalonia, the building then appears to be the paragon of a »dance factory«. Arribas describes the building as »a machine that transforms effectiveness into poetry and has been built to amaze the beholder«.

Der Name Gran Velvet bezieht sich auf die Bar-Diskothek Velvet mit der Arribas 1986 bekannt wurde. Beide Projekte wurden für denselben Auftraggeber ausgeführt. Arribas hatte in beiden Fällen »völlig freie Hand«. Das Gran Velvet ist zugleich Edel- und Großdiskothek. Die Namensgebung Gran Velvet erklärt Velvet zum Gattungsbegriff einer Spezies. Das Selbstzitat geht soweit, daß eine 1:1-Reproduktion des zentralen Raumes des Velvet in einer Glaskanzel aufgehängt im Gran Velvet schwebt. Diese Glaskanzel wird als VIP-Club und Cocktail-Bar genutzt. Sie ist schalldicht gegen die Diskothek abgeschirmt. Das Gran Velvet ist ein Multispace, ein Architekturtypus, der sich im Laufe der 80er und frühen 90er Jahre entwickelt hat. Er beinhaltet ein kompaktes Freizeitangebot und enthält Elemente der klassischen Dance Hall der 40er Jahre, der Diskothek der 70er Jahre und der Cocktailbar der 80er Jahre. Der multioptionale Nutzer verschiedener Alters- und Konsumgruppen kann hier die unterschiedlichsten Ereignisse passieren lassen und schließlich selbst flanieren. Unumgänglich hierfür sind die geräumigen und ausgedehnten Verkehrsflächen. Die Bars sind so groß angelegt, daß selbst bei Höchstbetrieb mit 5000 Besuchern der Zugriff auf den Drink rasch möglich ist. Die Außenschale zeigt eine Industrieästhetik, die durch das nächtliche Öffnen der Decke der zentralen Trommel eine spektakuläre Überhöhung erfährt. Wenn die Kuppel geöffnet wird, strömt die Diskothekenluft aus Bühnennebel und Rauch, mit hoher Luftfeuchtigkeit angereichert, wie aus dem Kühlturm eines Kraftwerkes aus. Dieses wird durch szenische Beleuchtung unterstützt. Das Gebäude wirkt wie der Inbegriff einer »Dance Factory« und ist somit ein Sinnbild der touristisch geprägten Ökonomie der katalanischen Küstenregion. Arribas beschreibt das Gebäude als eine Maschine, die »Poesie aus der Effektivität erschafft und die zum Staunen geschaffen ist.«

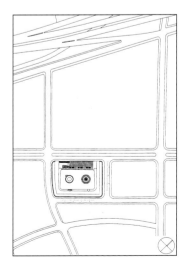

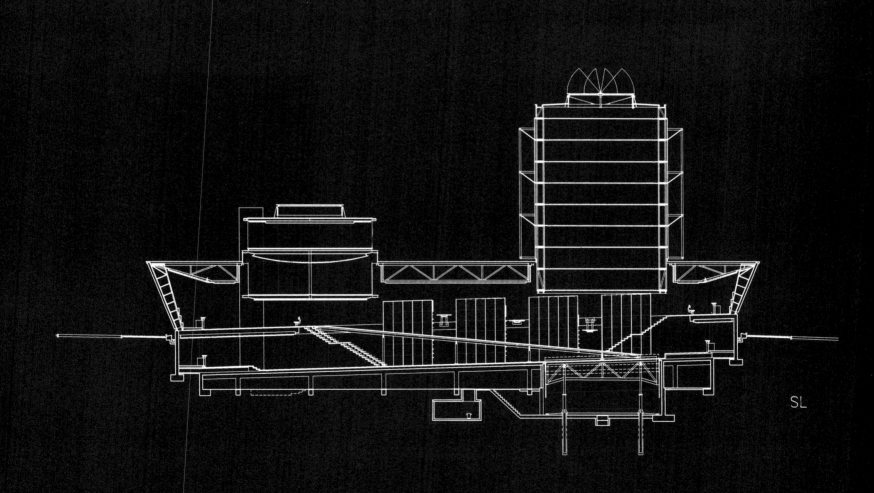

Das Gran Velvet spielt mit industrieller Ästhetik und Raumbildern. Die Toiletten wirken wie monumentale Kühlrohre. Die Trommel des Turmes erinnert an den Kühlturm der berühmten Szene von Terry Gilliams Film »Brazil«, auf den sich Arribas schon 1987 in seinem Projekt Network bezog.

The Gran Velvet plays with industrial aesthetics and spaces. The toilets look like enormous condenser tubes and the tambour of the tower reminds the famous shot of Terry Gilliam´s movie »Brazil«, to which Arribas had already referred in his project Network of 1987.

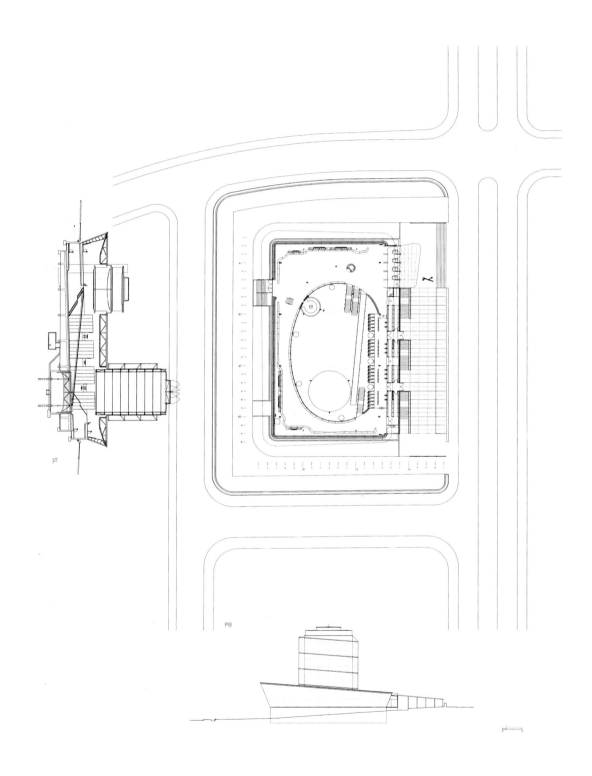

MCC
1995...

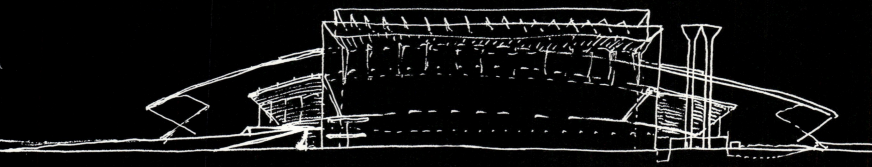

MCC

Multi-purpose building, showroom for Micro Compact Cars, and outlet for industrial use, 1995...

Mehrzweckgebäude, Micro Compact Car-Showroom und -Outlet für seriellen Einsatz, 1995 ...

The project clearly visualizes the distinction between its two major functions as showroom and multi-purpose building. The showroom consists of a high shelf that openly displays the Micro Compact Cars. The cars´ vertical (instead of a common horizontal) storage concisely emphasizes their »take-away« character. The wide, self-supporting hall embodies the all-under-one-roof-principle. The rather open architectural competition, won by Arribas against renowned firms such as Mario Botta and Nick Grimshaw, granted him a considerable degree of creative liberty he managed to fully employ.

Arribas was able to return to his experiences in designing multi-purpose leisure architecture (e.g. the Louie Vega Discotheque, 1988), as well as refer to works of temporary nature, such as the Spanish pavilion at the Frankfurt Book Fair (1994), and the stage buildings for the opening of the Olympics (1992). The light construction and the wide, self-supporting roof permit a wide variety of uses and provide a variable layout of the interior for additional commercial tenants. The »Superzeichencharakter« renders the building highly recognizable. MCC will obtain a strong public appeal within the buildings´ future neighborhoods, the arterial roads and industrial areas all over the world. Arribas shows what he has learned from Robert Venturi´s »Learning from Las Vegas«. He manages to vividly depict and restructure the genius loci. Most of all, however, this solution for unknown »non-places« previously proves convincing since it openly affirms and self-assuredly displays the car as an industrial product stripped of the false sentiment of representing an individual status symbol. Here, Michele De Lucchi´s »I believe in industry« has been turned into architecture.

Das Projekt unterscheidet klar und bildhaft die zwei zentralen Funktionen Showroom und Mehrzweckgebäude und stellt sie nebeneinander. Der Showroom wird durch ein Hochregal visualisiert, in dem die Micro Compact Cars weithin sichtbar gelagert werden. Durch die vertikale statt der bei PKW sonst üblichen horizontalen Lagerung wird der Charakter als Mitnahmeartikel, den das Auto bekommen soll, prägnant unterstrichen. Die weite, freitragende Halle hingegen verkörpert das Prinzip »alles unter einem Dach«. Der Wettbewerb, den Arribas gegen große Büros wie Mario Botta oder Nicholas Grimshaw gewann, ermöglichte durch die verhältnismäßig offene Ausschreibung eine große kreative Freiheit, die Arribas ganz ausschöpft.

Er konnte hier auf seine Erfahrungen mit Mehrzweck-Freizeitarchitekturen zurückgreifen (z.B. Louie Vega Diskothek, 1988) aber auch auf die Arbeit mit temporärer Architektur wie etwa dem Pavillon Spaniens auf der Buchmesse 1991 oder die Aufbauten für die Olympiaeröffnung (1992). Die Leichtbauweise und das weite freitragende Dach ermöglichen ein Maximum an unterschiedlichen Nutzungen und inneren Umbauten. Der Superzeichencharakter gibt dem Gebäude einen hohen Wiedererkennungswert und ermöglicht eine für MCC höchst werbewirksame dominante Position im künftigen Umfeld der Anlagen: den weltweiten Ausfallstraßen und Industriegebieten. Arribas zeigt hier, was er von Robert Venturi´s »Learning from Las Vegas« gelernt hat. Es gelingt ihm nicht nur den genius loci pointiert darzustellen und neu zu strukturieren. Seine Lösung für im voraus unbekannte Nichtorte überzeugt vor allem, indem sie sich offensiv zum Industrieprodukt Auto bekennt, ihm das falsche Sentiment des individuellen »Statusobjektes« nimmt und ihre eigene industrielle Eigenschaft selbstbewußt hervorkehrt. Dem »ich glaube an die Industrie«[1] von Michele De Lucchi wird hier von Arribas eine adäquate architektonische Visualisierung zur Seite gestellt.

---

1 Georg-Christof Bertsch: Videointerview zur Ausstellung »Citizen Office«, Vitra Design Museum, Weil am Rhein, 1994

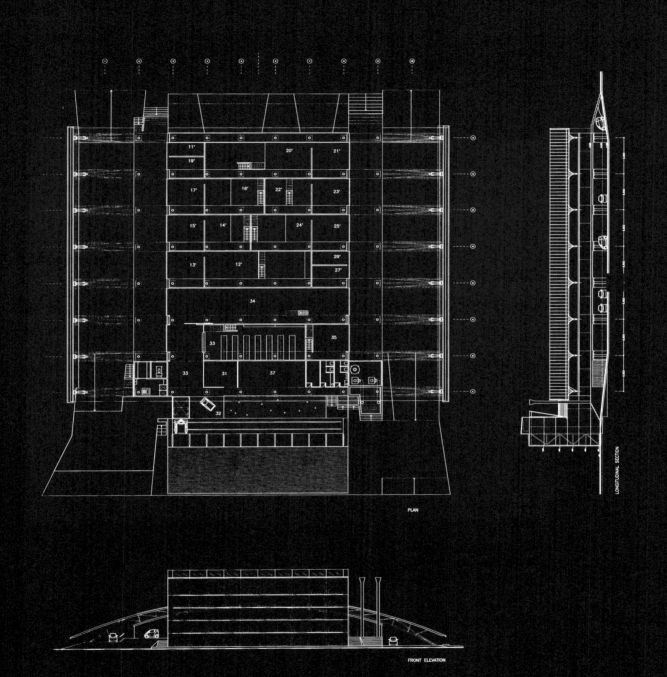

36

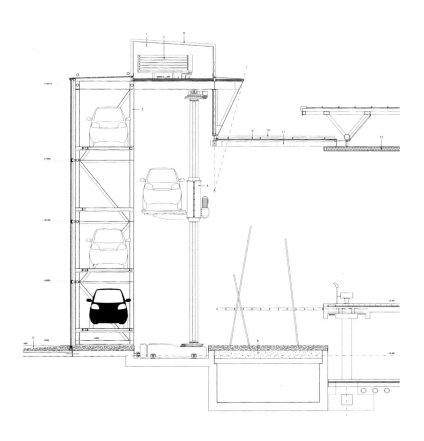

37

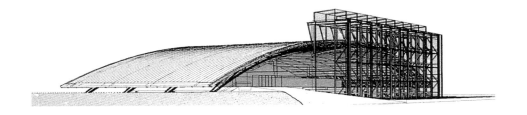

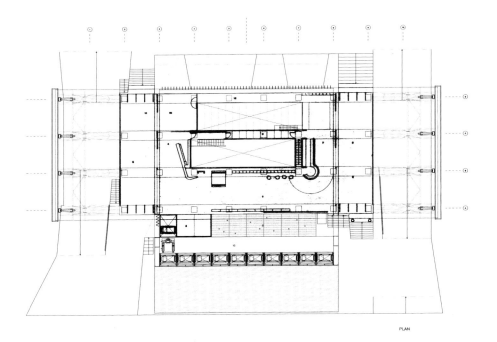

PLAN

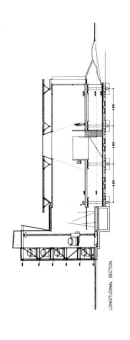

LONGITUDINAL SECTION

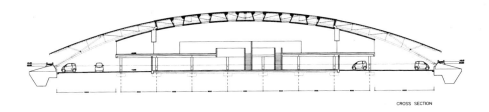

CROSS SECTION

MCC CENTER UPPER LEVEL

Sales of new cars
1. Open sales-show-room
2. Open space. Void
3. Presentation of cars
4. Shop for components/ access
5. Circulation space (annex)
6. Circulation space (annex)

Bistro
7. Cafe, Restaurant
8. Bistro front area

Component storage area
9. Corridor

Swatch watches
10. Shop
11. Front area
12. Corridor

Car storage area
13.

MEDINACELI
Barcelona, España, 1990-93

MEDINACELI

**Administration building for a transport company
Plaça Duc de Medinaceli on the corner of Carrer Ample,
Barcelona 1990-93**

Verwaltungsgebäude für eine Transportgesellschaft
Plaça Duc de Medinaceli Ecke Carrer Ample,
Barcelona 1990-93

Dieser alte Stadtpalast war durch mehrere unglückliche Teilrestaurierungen in einem beklagenswerten Zustand. Die Grundidee des Projektes besteht darin, das Gebäude äußerlich möglichst in seinen Urzustand zurückzuversetzen, es jedoch innerlich zu öffnen. Die Decken wurden zunächst komplett entfernt, außer jener zwischen Keller und Erdgeschoß. Die Fenster zum Innenhof, welche die tragenden Wände durchbrechen, wurden genau in die Achsen der Außenfenster gelegt. In den Kern des Innenhofes wurde anstelle der alten Treppe eine skulpturale Freitreppe gestellt. Diese Treppe vermittelt den Eindruck äußerster Leichtigkeit und die statische Illusion von der leichten Dachkonstruktion abgehängt zu sein.

Sie ist im Detail präzise durchgearbeitet und entpuppt sich als ein skulpturales Element mit vielfältigen Bezügen, von Oskar Schlemmer über Archipenko bis Richard Deacon. Diese monolithische Behandlung eines Elementes im Raum findet sich bis dahin bei Arribas nicht. Die plastische Durcharbeitung einer Treppe, wie sie schon dem frühen Projekt L'hort de les Monges (1986-87) auftaucht, nimmt hier sehr selbstbewußte Formen an. Diese Treppe genügt schlicht sich selbst, ohne freilich disfunktional zu sein. Es gelingt Arribas, mit der Treppe den Raum zu dominieren ohne ihn zu füllen. Sie verströmt Grazie ohne zerbrechlich zu wirken. Sie nimmt eine Sonderstellung in Arribas' Werk ein, da das ganze Gebäude zur Bühne für ihren Auftritt gemacht wird, vergleichbar nur dem Baukörper des zeitgleichen Marugame. Die Dachkonstruktion nimmt sich ebenfalls eine bemerkenswerte plastische Freiheit heraus, sie scheint sich schwingend über den Patio zu erheben. Diese Freitreppe ist zugleich Höhepunkt und Ende des skulpturalen Ansatzes von Arribas. Die Projektzeit 1990-93 markiert den Übergang von eine allegorischen zu einem eher rationalen Ansatz.

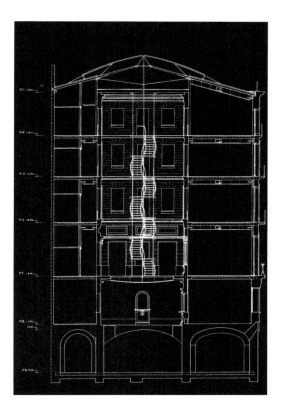

A number of ill-performed partial restorations had left this old city palace in a sad state. The project's general idea was then to restore the building's exterior to its original condition, while opening up the interior. All ceilings except the one between cellar and ground floor were taken down. The windows facing the inner court were arranged in the axes of the outer windows. The inner court's old staircase was replaced by a sculpturally modelled perron. This element gives an impression of utmost grace and creates the illusion that is suspended from the light roof construction.

Carefully worked out, the perron proves to be a sculptural element bearing manifold references to artists such as Oskar Schlemmer, Archipenko, or Richard Deacon. This monolithic treatment of one spatial element is a novelty with Arribas. The sculptural elaboration of a staircase, an approach which Arribas employed in the earlier project L'hort de les monges (1986-87), here yields highky self-confident forms. Far from being dysfunctional, this staircase simply appears to be self-sufficient. It dominates the space without crowding it, and eminates grace without appearing fragile. This sculpture takes up a special position within Arribas' work: the entire building has been rendered a stage for its entrance, comparable only to the construction of Marugame. The roof construction also takes remarkable spatial liberty as it seems to soar up, oscillating, over the patio. The perron, however, marks the climax but also the end of Arribas' sculptural style, with a transition from an allegorical to a more rational approach happening between 1990 and 1993.

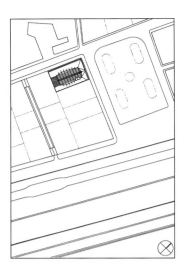
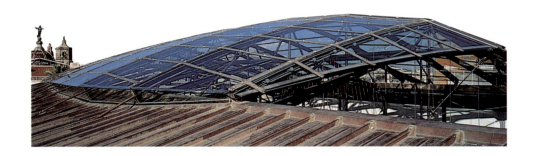
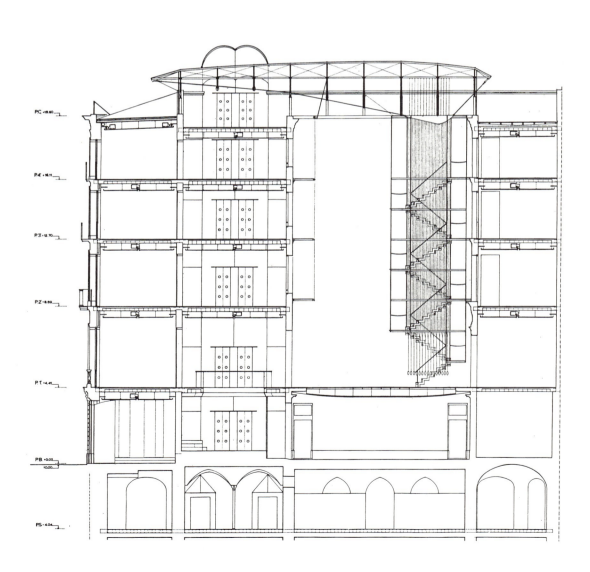

ESTANDARD
Barcelona, España, 1993

Estandard

**Bar for all-day service, café and club on first floor
Barcelona, Travessera de Gracia, 1993**

Bar für Ganztagsbetrieb, Café und Club im ersten Stock
Barcelona, Travessera de Gràcia, 1993

The Estandard turned out to be an amazing innovation within Barcelona's bar scene. Distinctly laid out and displaying an open and largely transparent structure, it formed a most obvious contrast to the opulent bars of the era. Hence Arribas rather firmly terms this bar a »post-1992-project«.

The building was originally constructed as a garage and was last used as a bingo hall. As it is typical for him, Arribas has acceded to the genius loci. The garage remains distinctly visible within the spacial elements. The ramp refers to another ramp formerly used in the garage; the sobriety of the construction's prior purpose is preserved. While he might have illustrated the building's historical aspect with allegorical elements a few years earlier, Arribas now prefers a reduced, somewhat more abstract form of reference.

The surrounding walls are made of concrete; acoustically and symbolically, they form an insulating shell. Consisting of metal, the partitions openly display their distinct function. By contrast, the wooden floors create a warm atmosphere.

Aside from preserving the former building's shell, the design particularly respects the supporting walls of the block facing the street. Its first floor houses the kitchen, and the ground floor provides a roomy entrance and lobby. The rear section's ceiling has been raised as far as possible; optimizing the visual effect of the upward opening, in order to optimize a number of supporting elements have been replaced by slim wire bracings. The facade is kept in a purposefully reduced, almost minimalist fashion. Nothing remains of the obsessive hunt for references from the movies, kitsch, and comics that was a trademark of Arribas' earlier projects. The Estandard is a programmatic statement.

Das Estandard war für die Barszene in Barcelona eine verblüffende Innovation. Klar strukturiert, mit einer offenen, weitgehend transparenten Struktur versehen, bildete es den größten denkbaren Kontrast zu den opulenten Bars der Zeit. Arribas bezeichnet diese Bar daher ausdrücklich als »nach-1992-Projekt«.

Das Gebäude war ursprünglich als Garage errichtet worden und wurde zuletzt als Bingohalle genutzt. Charakteristisch für Arribas ist das Eingehen auf den genius loci. Die Garage bleibt in den Raumelementen deutlich sichtbar. Die Rampe verweist auf eine andere, ehemalige Rampe der Garage, wobei die Nüchternheit der ehemaligen Nutzung erhalten bleibt. Hätte Arribas noch wenige Jahre zuvor den Ort mit allegorischen, narrativen Elementen der ehemaligen Nutzung »illustriert« so greift er hier zu einer reduzierteren, gleichsam abstrakteren Form der Darstellung.

Die umgebenden Wände sind aus Beton, sie bilden eine isolierende Schale, sowohl akustisch als auch symbolisch. Die Trennwände innerhalb dieser Schale sind aus Metall und stellen damit ihre andersartige Funktion deutlich zur Schau. Die Holzböden schaffen im Kontrast zu den Metallwänden, ein Gefühl von Wärme.

Das Projekt respektiert die Schale des ehemaligen Gebäudes und vor allem die tragenden Wände des der Straße zugewandten Blocks. Die Küche liegt im ersten Geschoß dieses Blocks. Sein Erdgeschoß wird als geräumige Eingangs- und Verkehrssituation genutzt. Die Höhe im hinteren Bereich wird weitmöglichst geöffnet. Einige tragende Elemente wurden zu diesem Zweck durch schlanke Drahtverspannungen ersetzt, um die optische Öffnung nach oben zu optimieren.

Die Fassade ist bewußt reduziert, fast minimalistisch gehalten. Nichts ist mehr zu spüren von der obsessiven Jagd nach Referenzen aus Film, Kitsch und Comic, die für die früheren Projekte von Arribas so charakteristisch waren. Estandard ist eine programmatische Aussage.

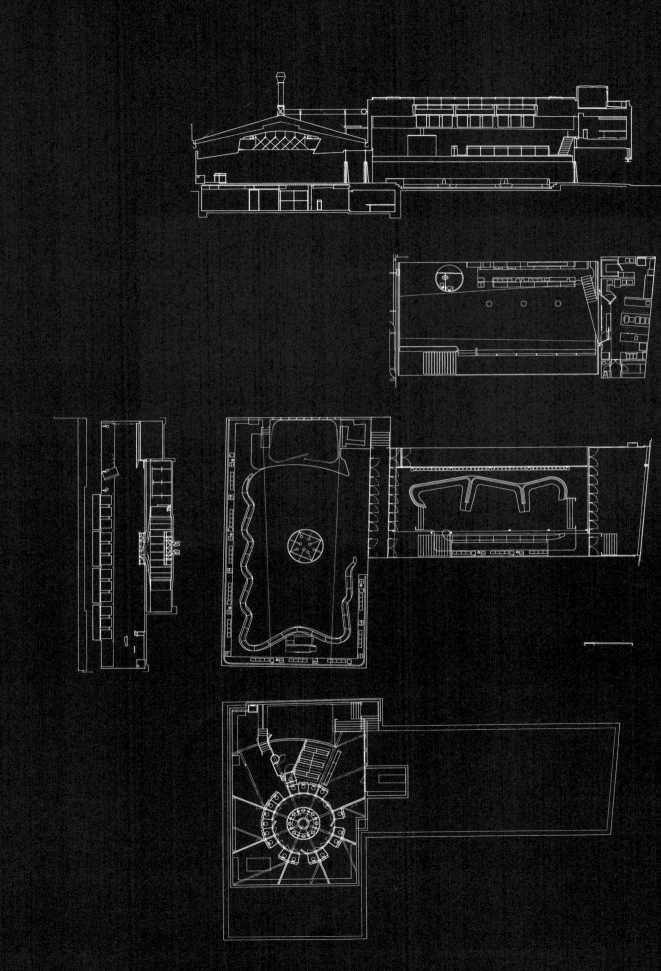

Cosmo Hall
Osaka, Japan, 1995

COSMO HALL

Cosmo Hall, World Trade Center Osaka, Japan, 1994-95

Cosmo Hall, World Trade Center, Osaka, Japan, 1994-95

Cosmo Hall is located on the 48th and 49th stories of the Osaka World Trade Center, one of the most expensive and exclusive places in the world. Needless to say, the astonishing thing about this project by Alfredo Arribas is not that it involved designing a buffet restaurant. The truly delicate side of the project was to create a space that can be used for both Shinto and Christian religious ceremonies, as well as host all kinds of conferences and symposiums. It is considered a real luxury to get married here; at 200 meters above ground level it is the loftiest place of matrimony in Japan. As a result of all this, the multi-purpose premises had to fulfill three conditions: 1. embody traditional Japanese elements that would create a dignified setting for Shinto ceremonies, while at the same time representing the modern side of Japan for commercial events, 2. be appropriate for Christian services, satisfying their requirements for seclusion and intimacy, and 3. provide structures for handling logistics, especially in terms of food and drink, that would also hold up under the onslaught of even the largest events. Arribas subdivided the total available area into two banquet halls, a buffet restaurant, and a multi-purpose ceremony room. He concentrated the functional aspects of each room in the smallest possible space, thus ensuring that those functions would not be disturbed and simultaneously creating large areas on which peolpe can circulate, despite intensive use. These large areas lend the overall construction a certain openess and – in a crowded country like Japan – a sense of luxury. The extremely narrow entrances, accesses and the vestibules enhance the expansive interior proportions. Those who enter Cosmo Hall are given an exaggerated impression of solemn breadth, calm forms, and equilibrium. The parabolic layout of the glass partitions of the wedding chamber eliminates any bulkiness and provides for a maximum degree of transparency, with curtains availabale should more privacy be desired. The true achievement of this construction is the define efficiency of its layout; there is a certain magic in its different perspectives and in the sequence of the rooms. This, together with graphic ceiling and floor structures that are reminiscent of tatami mats, lends the necessary traditional gravity to a modern ambiance. The architecture manages to bridge cultural gaps, and to unite diverging economic, religious, and traditional needs.

Die Cosmo Hall befindet sich im 48. und 49. Stock des World Trade Center Osaka, an einem der teuersten und exklusivsten Plätze der Welt. Nicht die Aufgabe, ein Buffet-Restaurant zu gestalten, ist das Verblüffende dieses Projektes von Alfredo Arribas. Die eigentlich delikate Seite des Auftrages war die Gestaltung eines Raumes für religiöse Festlichkeiten sowohl der Shinto-Religion als auch des Christentums. Zusätzlich finden hier Konferenzen aller Art und Vortragsveranstaltungen statt. Hier, 200 Meter über dem Boden, zu heiraten, im höchsten Trauungsraum des Inselreiches, gilt als wahrer Luxus. Die Mehrzweck-Räumlichkeiten mußten also drei wesentlichen Ansprüchen genügen: 1. sowohl traditionelles Japan verkörpern, um für Shinto-Festlichkeiten den würdigen Rahmen zu bieten als auch modernes Japan darstellen, um kommerziellen Veranstaltungen zu genügen; 2. christlichen liturgischen Ansprüchen genügen und deren Bedarf an Zurückgezogenheit und Intimität befriedigen; 3. logistische Strukturen bieten, welche auch bei größten Veranstaltungen, vor allem im gastronomischen Bereich, dem Ansturm Stand halten. Arribas unterteilte das Gesamtareal in zwei Bankettshallen, ein Buffetrestaurant und einen Mehrzweckraum für Feierlichkeiten. Er konzentrierte die Funktionen jeweils auf möglichst kleinem Raum. Damit entzerrte er die Funktionen und ermöglichte zugleich trotz der intensiven Nutzungen große Verkehrsflächen, die dem Gesamtkomplex eine gewisse Offenheit und - im beengten Japan - das Flair des Luxus geben. Zugunsten dieser Weite im Innern werden die Eingangs- und Zugangswege sowie die Vestibüle räumlich äußerst knapp bemessen. Dadurch entsteht beim Betreten ein übersteigerter Eindruck feierlicher Weite, formaler Ruhe und Ausgeglichenheit. Besonders die parabolischen Grundrisse der gläsernen Trennwände beim Trauungssaal nehmen dem Raum alles Sperrige und schaffen eine maximale Transparenz, die bei Bedarf durch Vorhänge reduziert werden kann. Die eigentliche Leistung liegt hier in der sicheren Effizienz des Grundrisses, der eine gewisse Magie der Durchblicke und Raumabfolgen ermöglicht. Dies in Kombination mit den an Tatami-Matten erinnernden graphischen Strukturen von Decke und Boden gibt dem modernen Ambiente die nötige traditionelle Gravität. Dadurch gelingt es der Architektur, kulturelle Brücken zu schlagen und divergierenden Ansprüchen von Ökonomie, Religion und Brauchtum zu vereinen.

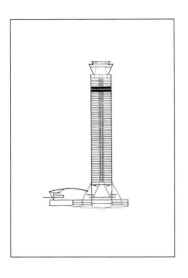

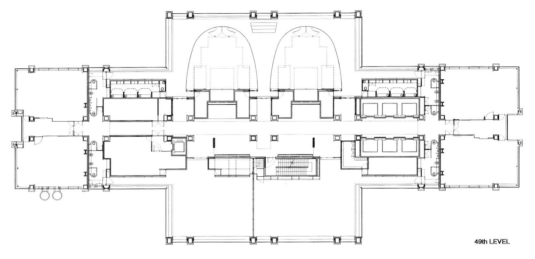

49th LEVEL

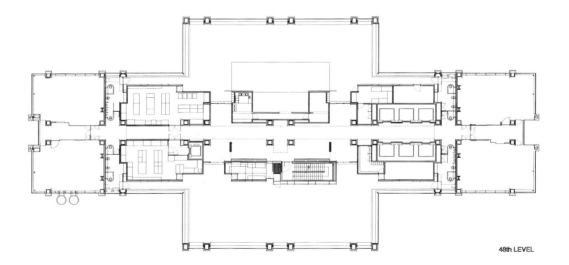

48th LEVEL

EURONET
Frankfurt, Deutschland, 1995 …

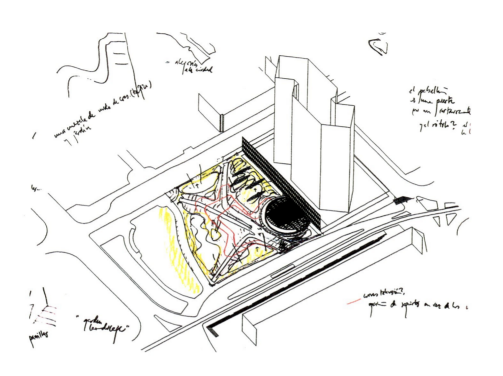

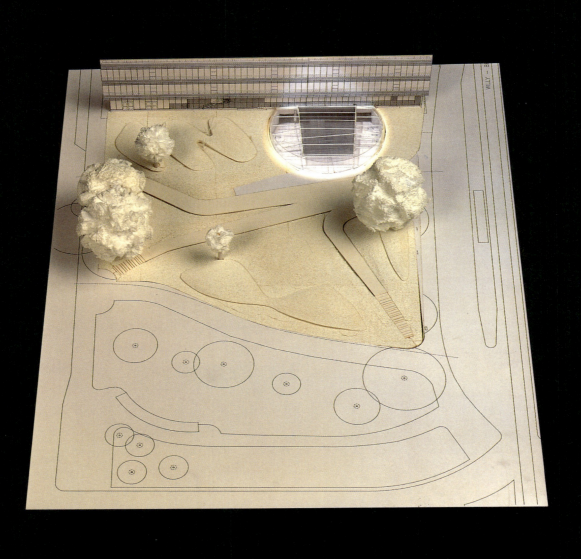

EURONET

Multi-purpose-complex housing a gastronomic landscape and a shopping mall with luxury and semi-luxury goods, Frankfurt am Main, 1995

Mehrzweck-Komplex aus Gastronomie-Landschaft, Shopping mall mit Angeboten für den täglichen Bedarf sowie Mall mit Angeboten für den gehobenen Bedarf, Frankfurt am Main, 1995

The former BfG tower at Willy-Brandt-Platz in Frankfurt is one of the city's most elegant skyscrapers It was purchased by the GRUNDWERT-FONDS of DEGI Deutsche Gesellschaft für Immobilienfond mbH and recast by Köllmann GmbH. The European Monetary Institute, the predecessor of the Central European Bank, was secured as its main tenant. Arribas was commissioned to completely redesign the ground floor and basement (Euronet), a task bearing urbanistic responsibility, as the miserable previous layout had led to the outright desertion of the mall shops and their environment. Moreover, this happened in spite of the fact that the building has its own subway station and streetcar stop, and is situated 200 meters from the very heart of the city in a well-to-do shopping area, near the opera, ballet, and city theater. The problematic basement situation was resolved by generously expanding the Netfood area. Shaped like the segment of a circle, a winter garden provides many of the subterranean areas with natural light. The inner structure opened up considerable so that people may circulate throughout.

The materials used in construction of the Netfood include many open concrete and metal surfaces, emphaszing the functional and pragmatic aspects of the professional gastronomic context. A fresh, straightforward aesthetic is used to appeal to the very young target group. Materials conveying an »honest« vocabulary, as in the »Gran Velvet«, 1993, prevail. This »honesty« is an element which is extremly important for the young and youngest customers. An example of this is the almost irritatingly smooth, wide surfaces of the Schirn Café, combined with open sandstone, which create a room existing not primarily for its own end, but instead providing the space for whatever is to happen within. (This reveals the extent to which Arribas has already distanced himself from works like »Torre de Avila«, 1990, or »Barna Crossing«, 1989.)

Das ehemalige BfG-Haus am Willy-Brandt-Platz, eines der baulich elegantesten Hochhäuser der Frankfurter City, wurde von dem GRUNDWERT-FONDS der DEGI Deutsche Gesellschaft für Immobilienfonds mbH erworben und von der Köllmann GmbH umgebaut. Als Hauptmieter wurde das Europäische Währungsinstitut (EWI), der Vorläufer der Europäischen Zentralbank, gewonnen. Arribas wurde mit der Aufgabe betraut, das Erdgeschoß sowie das Basement komplett umzugestalten (Euronet). Die Aufgabe hat insofern städtebauliche Aspekte, da durch die zuvor miserable Innenarchitektur dieser Bereiche eine regelrechte Verödung der Ladenlokale und des Umfeldes stattgefunden hatte. Dies geschah zudem trotz der optimalen Anbindung des Gebäudes mit eigenen U- und Trambahn-Stationen, 200 Metern Fußweg zum absoluten Zentrum der Stadt, unmittelbarer Nachbarschaft zu Oper, Ballett, Schauspiel sowie einem ausgesprochen kaufkräftigen Umfeld.

Die problematische Basement-Lage wurde nun durch das weite Öffnen des gastronomischen Bereiches (Netfood) gelöst. Ein Wintergarten in Form eines Kreissegmentes versorgt einen großen Teil der unterirdischen Räume mit natürlichem Licht. Die innere Struktur wurde weitgehend entkernt und geöffnet, um in allen Bereichen den Verkehrsströmen freien Lauf zu gewähren.

Die Materialwelt des Netfood zeigt viele offene Beton und Metalloberflächen und betont die Funktionalität und Pragmatik des professionellen gastromischen Zusammenhanges.

Die sehr junge Zielgruppe wird über die ungekünstelte, gradlinige Ästhetik angesprochen. Materialanmutungen wie aus dem »Gran Velvet« (1993) mit ihrem »ehrlichen« Vokabular herrschen vor. Dieser elementare Faktor, die »Ehrlichkeit« spielt für die jungen und jüngsten Zielgruppen eine nicht zu unterschätzende Rolle. Schon im Schirn-Café hatten die zunächst befremdlich glatten, weiten Oberflächen in Kombination mit offenem Sandstein das unverwechselbare Klima eines Raumes geschaffen, der nicht vorrangig selbst »ist«, sondern der Raum gibt, für das was auch immer in ihm geschehen mag. (Hier zeigt sich die enorme Distanz, die Arribas schon heute zu Werken wie »Torres de Avila« (1990) oder »Barna Crossing« (1989) gewonnen hat.)

Charakteristisch und programmatisch für die offenen Formen ist die lange wellenförmige Bar des Zentralbereiches im gastronomischen Sektor. Sie erinnert an die langestreckte Bar des »Estandard« (1993). Die lange Bar hatte sich auch schon im ebenfalls in Frankfurt realisierten »Schirn-Café« (1993) bewährt. Die lange Theke hat Arribas unter anderem von der spezifischen sozialen Situation der langen Bänke in den Apfelweinkneipen Frankfurts abgeleitet. Die Kombination zwischen dem einzelnen Barhocker auf der einen und der ausgesprochen langen Bar auf der anderen Seite hat überdies mehrere logistische Vorteile für den Service hinter der Bar. Vor allem in den Stoßzeiten um Mittag und nach Feierabend lassen sich mit relativ wenig Personal größte Mengen Mahlzeiten, Snacks, Sandwiches etc. verkaufen, ohne daß der Gast drängeln oder anstehen muß. Und ohne daß zu großer Streß beim Personal aufkommt, da die lineare Barsituation gut überschaubar ist. Ausdrücklich vermieden wird die für den online-Betrieb charakteristische, demütigende Schlange vor der »Essensausgabe«.

Die klassische spanische Tapas-Bar mit ihren Tresenauslagen wird hier mit Elementen des amerikanischen Diners und regionalspezifischen Gewohnheiten verschmolzen. Im Gesamtbereich des Netfood werden internationale Speisen in einer innovativen Kombination von Marché-, Take-away, Home delivery und Bar-Gastronomie angeboten. Neben der Bar gibt es Bistrot-, Restaurant- und Cocktailbar-Zonen auf insgesamt 1500 qm. Die unmittelbare Nähe zum EWI mit ihren weltweiten Vernetzungen gab unter anderem den Anstoß für den Betreiber, Kofler, Inn Side & Partner, den Netfood an alle verfügbaren Computer-Netzwerke anzuschließen, um Bestellungen, »virtual parties« und »virtual plazas« zu ermöglichen, die in dieser Form bislang noch nicht existierten. Die Inbetriebnahme des Gesamtkomplexes wird, das kann schon heute gesagt werden, zu einer Belebung des gesamten Umfeldes des Eurotowers beitragen. Die Öffnung des Publikumsverkehrs von der zentralen Hauptwache Frankfurts nach Westen, die in den letzten Jahren begonnen hat, wird dadurch verstärkt werden.

Diese »städtebauliche« Einflußnahme von Arribas - schon durch den verblüffenden Erfolg des Schirn-Cafés (»Frankfurts neue Mitte«, Hartwin Möhrle, Chefredakteur Journal Frankfurt) eingeleitet -, wird hier in einer komplexeren Aufgabe fortgesetzt.

A long, wave-shaped bar in the central area´s gastronomic section epitomizes the project´s open forms. It is reminiscent of the seemingly endless bar of the »Estandard« (1993). A bar of similar dimensions had already proved its worth in the Schirn Café, also realized in Frankfurt (1993). Besides, the long bar was inspired by the specific social situation in Frankfurt´s cider pubs with their long benches. The combination of single bar stools and an usually long bar also has serveral logistic advantages for bar services. Meals, Snacks, Sandwiches, etc. can be served en masse by relatively few people without customers having to shove or queue, even during midday, evening peak hours. Easy to survey, the linear bar situation also makes things easier for the employees. A humiliating »bread line«, typical of on-line operations, is clearly avoided.

Here, the classic Spanish tapas bar, with the food displayed in the counter, is blended with elements of American diners and local habits. As a whole, the Netfood features an international variety of meals in an innovative combination of »marché« (buffet-style), take-away, home delivery, and bar gastronomy. Apart from the bar, there are the bistro, restaurant, and cocktail bar zone which together cover an area of 1500 m^2. The proximity of the EWI with its worldwide networks prompted operators Kofler, Inn Side & Partner to link the Network to all available computer networks. This permits customers to order as of yet unpreceded »virtual parties« and »virtual plazas«. When the overall complex begins operations, it will unquestionably contribute to the stimulation of the Eurotower neighborhood. Continuing the trend of recent years, the opening of Frankfurt´s Hauptwache to traffic heading west will be opened even further.

The stunning sucess of the Schirn Cafe was only the beginning of Arribas´ »urbanistic« intervention (»Frankfurt´s new center«, according to Hartwin Möhrle, chief editor of Journal Frankfurt), which being continued here as part of a more complex assignment.

Der Entwurf folgt einem städteplanerischen Ansatz.

The design follows ideas of urban planning.

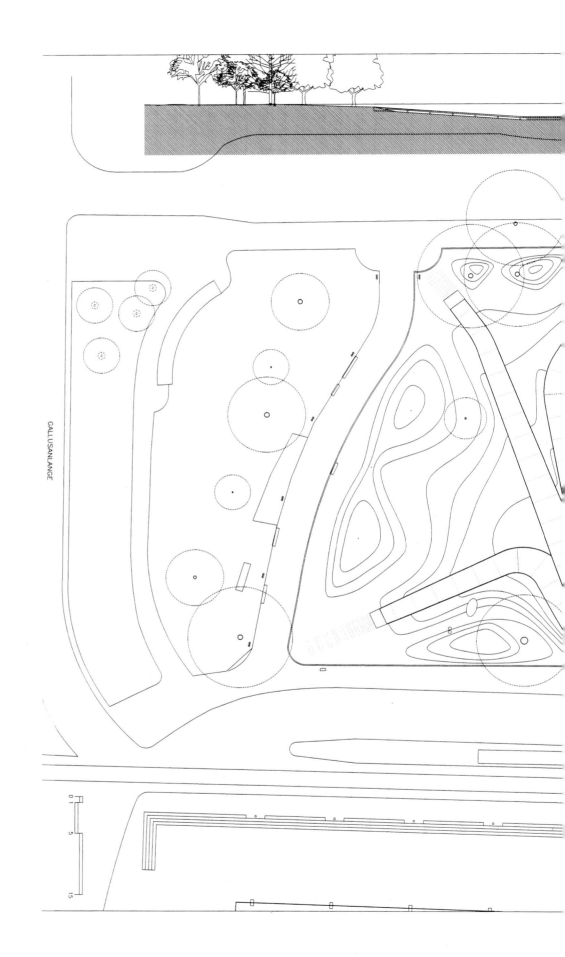

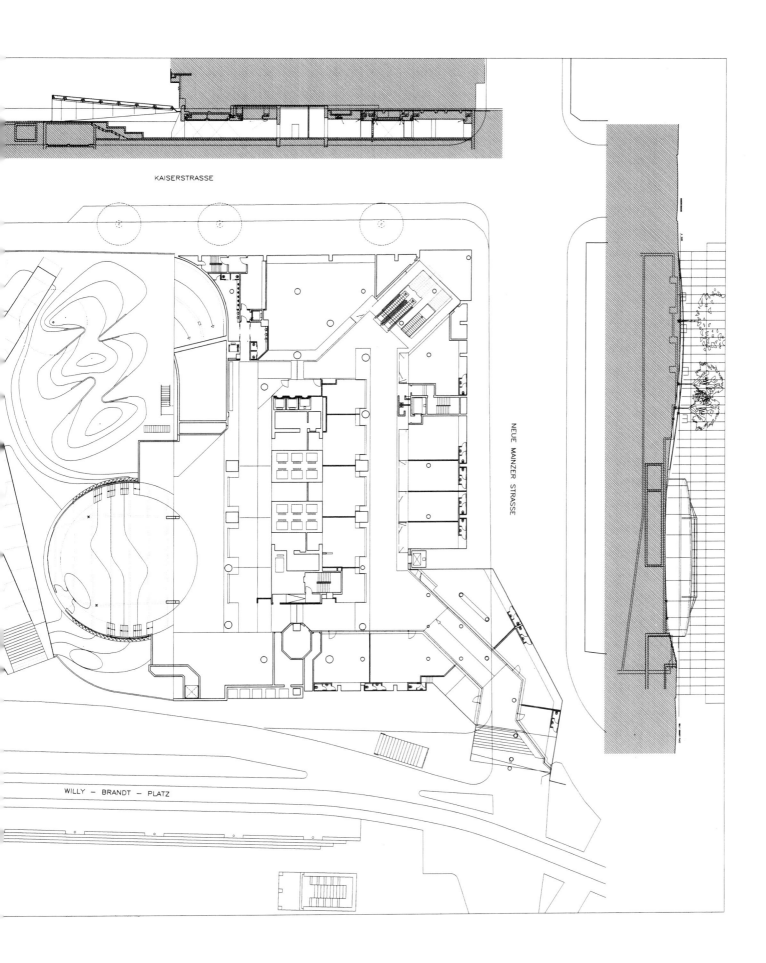

Design Objekte/Design Objects
1994-95

»Torna« & **»Sputnik«**, Producer: Ediciones Ilimitadas, 1992

»Bola Sofa«, Producer: Casas, 1994
»Zenio«, Producer: bd Ediciones de Diseño, 1992

Design Objects

1994-95

»Una Chair«
Producer: Amat
1995

Spaces designed by Arribas cannot be furnished. They are complete from the outset, down to the tiniest screw. Naturally, this includes the furniture as well. For Arribas, a naked room does not count; the design object in itself is of no value to him if it is not built in as a composite element of a room. Likewise, a room devoid of people does not exist in his eyes. His rooms derive their function through their interaction with people. The design objects are elements that orient a person within the room, but which on the other hand also offer the opportunity to modify the room according to individual tastes. The design objects and the room exist in a kind of symbiosis. As Arribas sees it, nothing could more reprehensible stuffing a room with cheap goods as part of a price-conscious advertisement. This would be killing the room. In many of his works, such as Barna Crossing (1989), Torres de Avila (1990), Velvet (1986) or Network (1987), Arribas designed furniture specially for the project. In others, such as the Schirn Café, he used furniture that he had designed for other, similar projects (in this case, the Sputnik bar stool from the Estandard). Only very recently has he begun to produce furniture that is not bound to any particular room (for example, the Fregoli chair, designed for Italien luxury goods producer Sawaya & Moroni). Arribas' established image as an architect and interior designer is of use to this new generation of design objects. The new objects are increasingly imbued with the power to take their place in any room. Also contributing to this effect is an unusual style which subtly rejects traditional proportions. However, they are not to be included in the ranks of the architect-furniture of Le Corbusier, O.M. Ungers, or Norman Foster, for Arribas' objects are not aimed at propagating an architectural program. Nor are they intended to illustrate any architectonic principles, as they were conceived for their own sake. In this respect, they stand out from the Arribas' previous furniture designs, which were always part of an architectural program.

Die Räume von Arribas kann man nicht möblieren, denn sie sind von vornherein bis hin zur kleinsten Schraube entworfen. Dazu gehören die Möbel wie selbstverständlich. Der nackte Raum gilt Arribas nichts, das Designobjekt allein hat für ihn keinen Wert, solange es nicht in einem Raum kompositorisch eingebaut ist. Der Raum ohne Menschen existiert für ihn ebenfalls nicht. Seine Räume funktionieren im Wechselspiel mit den Menschen. Die Designobjekte sind Elemente, die den Menschen im Raum organisieren, die ihm andererseits aber auch die Möglichkeit geben, den Raum individuell zu modifizieren. Die Designobjekte und der Raum bilden eine Symbiose. Nichts wäre für Arribas verwerflicher, als in einer an Preisen orientierten Ausschreibung die Räume mit Billigware vollzuräumen. Man würde den Raum damit liquidieren. In vielen Fällen, wie dem Barna Crossing (1989), Torres de Avila (1990), Velvet (1986), Network (1987) entwarf Arribas Möbel speziell für ein Projekt. In anderen Fällen, wie dem Schirn-Café, wurden Möbel die er für andere, vergleichbare Projekte entworfen hatte, eingesetzt (in diesem Fall der Barhocker Sputnik aus dem Estandard). Erst in jüngster Zeit entstehen Möbel, die an keinen bestimmten Raum gebunden sind (z.B. der Stuhl Fregoli, 1995 für den noblen italienischen Möbelhersteller Sawaya & Moroni). Diese neue Generation von Designobjekten können mittlerweile schon mit dem etablierten Image des Architekten und Innenarchitekten Arribas operieren. Ihnen wohnt die raumgreifende Kraft bereits in statu nascendi inne. Eine seltsame Stilistik, die sich herkömmlichen Proportionen in feinen Nuancen verweigert, ermöglicht diesen Effekt zusätzlich. Sie sind jedoch nicht ohne weiteres in die Gruppe der Architekten-Möbel von Le Corbusier über O.M. Ungers bis Norman Foster einzuordnen, da sie keine architektonische Programmatik propagieren wollen. Sie wollen keine architektonischen Prinzipien illustrieren, da sie an und für sich gedacht sind. Insofern scheren sie auch aus der Reihe der älteren Möbelentwürfe von Arribas aus, die stets Bestandteil der architektonischen Programme der Projekte waren.

»Fregoli Chair«
Producer: Sawaya & Moroni, 1995

»Pila Chair and Armchair«,
Producer: Casas, 1995

»**Copa Stool**«, Producer: Casas, 1994

ALFREDO ARRIBAS

Geboren 1954 in Barcelona. Architekt der Technischen Schule für Architektur (ETSAB) in Barcelona (1977). Seit 1987 Professor an der ETSAB sowie an der Designschule Elisava, Barcelona, wo er auch als Koordinator des Fachbereichs Design arbeitet und seit 1990 Mitglied des Direktoriums ist. Während dieser Jahre aktive Zusammenarbeit mit dem FAD, Verband der Industriedesigner zur Förderung der Angewandten Künste. Von 1982 bis 1986 war er Direktor der INFAD, Vereinigung der Innenarchitekten der FAD, 1986 - 1988 Vizepräsident des FAD, 1989 erhielt er für seine beruflichen Leistungen die Goldmedaille des FAD.

1986 gründete er zusammen mit Miguel Morte das Architekturbüro Alfredo Arribas Arquitectos Asociados (AAAA). Seither haben beide eine Vielzahl von Architektur- und Inneneinrichtungsprojekten durchgeführt. Besonders hervorzuheben sind: Designschule Elisava, Casa Pastor, Network Café, Velvet Bar, das Geschäft Francisco Valiente in Madrid, das Restaurant L'Hort de les Monges, Clik dels Nens im Wissenschaftsmuseum Barcelona, die Louie Vega-Freizeitanlage und das Kaufhaus Rosa in Mercabarna (Barcelona). Diese Projekte sind sämtlich ausgezeichnet worden oder standen in der Endausscheidung für Auszeichnungen mit Preisen wie dem des FAD, dem Preis der Stadt Barcelona, EDIM, dem Preis der freien Gemeinde Madrid und dem Bonaplata-Preis für technologische Innovation in der Architektur. 1988 vertrat Arribas Spanien auf der Biennale von Barcelona in der Kategorie »Junge europäische Architekten«.

1989 wurde er zusammen mit Aldo Rossi, Ettore Sottsass, Gaetano Pesce und Shiro Kuramata eingeladen, am Il-Palazzo-Projekt in Fukuoka/Japan teilzunehmen. Gemeinsam mit einem jungen Team schöpferischer Architekten aus Barcelona entwarf er eine »Multi-Space-Kreuzung«, die sich als wegweisend für seine späteren internationalen Projekte erwies.

1988 und 1991 gewann sein Büro folgende Wettbewerbe: Erweiterung des Wissenschaftsmuseums Barcelona, Spanischer Pavillon auf der Frankfurter Buchmesse 1991, Neugestaltung von Schornstein und Silos der alten Sanson-Werke in Sant Just Desvern, Vergnügungspark Nuova Fibilandia in Rimini/Italien.

Von da an wechselten sich Arbeiten in Katalonien mit internationalen Projekten ab. So entwarf er die Konzerthalle von Lledia, die Bar Torres des Avila in Barcelona, den Segovia-Golfclub bei Tokio, die Acuarinto Children Hall in Nagasaki und das Café der Schirn Kunsthalle in Frankfurt am Main. In all diesen Jahren wurden seine Entwürfe in den angesehensten spanischen und internationalen Architektur- und Designzeitschrften sowie in zahlreichen Büchern veröffentlicht. Ein Kompendium der Arbeiten aus dieser Zeit findet sich in: »Alfredo Arribas. Architecture and Design Works 1988-1992«, Ernst Wasmuth Verlag, Tübingen; mit Texten von Georg Christof Bertsch und einem Vorwort von Oscar Tusquets.

1992 entwarf er die Ausstattung und das »Bühnenbild« für die Feiern zu den Olympischen Spielen von Barcelona. Danach wandte er sich verstärkt Großprojekten zu, so daß der Schwerpunkt sich in den architektonischen Bereich verlagerte.

Von seinen jüngeren und gegenwärtigen Projekten seien folgende erwähnt: Hirai-Museum für zeitgenössische Kunst in Marugame. Mit diesem Projekt gewann er folgende Preise: Japan Commercial Space Design Award, Good Design Lightning Award of Japan, Kagawa Society of Architects and Building Engineers. Weiterhin der Multi-Komplex Estandard in Barcelona, ein Hotel am Murasaki-Fluß in Kita-Kyishu, die Diskothek Gran Velvet, Spin Spaces auf der Spitze des Fernsehturms Shanghai, der 48. und 49. Stock des World Trade Center in Osaka, eine Recycling-Anlage für Autoreifen zur Gewinnung elektrischer Energie, ein Kraftwerk, sowie das Hung-Kuo-Gebäude mit Einkaufspassage und Wohnungen in Shanghai, China. Als Projekte aus allerjüngster Zeit in Deutschland sind zu nennen: das Euronet mit Einkaufspassage, Großrestaurant, gläsernem Pavillon sowie Garten im Eurotower-Gebäude, Frankfurt am Main, sowie die Ausstattung des TAT Theater und seines Theatercafés, ebenfalls in Frankfurt am Main.

Im Mai 1995 gewann Alfredo Arribas zwei wichtige internationale Wettbewerbe: den ersten Preis ausgeschrieben durch MCC (Micro Compact Car Corporation, ein joint venture zwischen Mercedes Benz und Swatch), für den Entwurf der neuen Compact Car Verkaufszentren in Europa. Ein von Lufthansa ausgelobter Preis für die Neugestaltung von Warte- und Abfertigungsbereichen in Flughäfen. Dieses Projekt befindet sich zur Zeit noch im Prozeß.

Arribas war und ist mit Ausstellungen und Lesungen bei zahlreichen nationalen und internationalen Institutionen zu Gast, darunter: Design Museum (London) 1991, Architektur Zentrum (Wien) 1991, Architectural Association School of Architecture

Born in Barcelona in 1954. 1977 Architect of the Technical School of Architecture of Barcelona (ETSAB). Since 1987 he has held a professorship both at ETSAB and at the Elisava School of Design, of which he is also the coordinator for the Department of Interior Design. Since 1990, he has also been a member of the Board of Directors.

During these years, he actively collaborated with the FAD (Association of Industrial Design for the Development of Decorative Arts). From 1982 to 1985 he was president of INFAD (Association of Interior Designers of FAD), and from 1986 to 1988, Vice-president of FAD. In 1989 he was awarded the FAD Gold Medal in recognition of his professional achievement.

In 1986, together with Miguel Morte, he established the company Alfredo Arribas Arquitectos Asociados (AAAA). Since then, they have been intensively active in numerous works, alternating between the fields of architecture and interior design. Amongst others, the most outstanding works are: the Elisava School of Design, Casa Pastor, Network Cafe, Velvet Bar, the Francisco Valiente store in Madrid, the restaurant L´Hort de les Monges, Clik dels Nens in the Barcelona Museum of Science, the Louie Vega leisure complex, and the Warehouse Rosa in Mercabarna (Barcelona). All of these works are notable as having won prizes or having been finalists for prizes such as the FAD Award, the Cuidad de Barcelona Award for Technological Innovation in Architecture. In 1988 he represented Spain in the Barcelona II Biennal in the category of »Young European Architects«.

In 1989 he was invited together with Aldo Rossi, Ettore Sottsass, Gaetano Pesce and Shiro Kuramata, to participate in the II Palazzo project in Fukuoka, Japan. Surrounded by young creative Barcelona architects, he created the multi-space Crossing, which was decisive in projecting his work on an international level.

In 1988 and 1991 his studio was awarded the following projects: building the extension of the Barcelona Science Museum, the Spanish Pavilion of the Frankfurt Book Fair in 1991, remodelling the chimney and silos of the old Sanson Factory in Sant Just Desvern, and the Amusement Park Nuova Fibilandia in Rimini, Italy.

From then on, he alternated his creations in Catalonia with works and projects in various countries. During this period he created the Concert Hall Wonder in Lledia, the Torres de Avila Bar in Barcelona, the Segovia Golf Club near Tokyo, the Acuarinto in Nagasaki and the Schirn-Cafe of the Schirn Kunsthalle in Frankfurt am Main.

Troughout the course of these years, his work was published extensively in the most prestigious national and international magazines on architecture and design, as well as in numerous books. A compendium of his works is found in the monograph »Alfredo Arribas. Architecture and Design Works 1986-1992«, put out by the German publishing company Ernst Wasmuth Verlag, Tübingen, with texts by Georg-C. Bertsch and a prologue by Oscar Tusquets.

In 1992 he designed the scenery and architectural elements for the ceremonies of the Barcelona Olympic Games. Subsequently, the scale of his projects became progressively larger, and he began leaning towards more specifically architectural subjects.

Some of Arribas´ most important recent works include the Hirai Museum of Spanish Contemporary Art in Marugame. (in 1994 this project received the following awards: Japan Commercial Space Design Award, Good Design Lightning Award of Japan, Kagawa Society of Architects and Building Engineers); the multi-complex Estandard in Barcelona; a hotel beside the Murasaki River in Kita-Kyishu; Gran Velvet discotheque; Spin Spaces in the top of the Shanghai TV Communication Tower; the 49th and 50th floors of the World Trade Center in Osaka, a Recycling Plant of Tyres for Energy; and the Hung-Kuo Building, a shopping and residential center in Shanghai, China. Two very recent projects based in Germany, are the Euronet, a shopping mall, glass pavilion and garden in the Eurotower Building, and the installation of the TAT theater and its coffee hall in the Bockenheimer Depot, both in Frankfurt/Main.

On May 1995, he awarded two important competitions: 1st prize of the MCC (Micro Compact Car Corporation, a joint venture between Mercedes Benz and Swatch), to design the New Compact Car Sales Centers in all European Cities. And a competition held by Lufthansa for their new airport lounges; this is still in process.

Various national and international institutions have invited him to exhibit his works and to give lectures. He has also been asked to serve on various international juries of architecture and design. The most notable ones are: Design Museum (London) 1991, Architektur Zentrum (Vienna) 1991, Architectural Association School of Architecture (London) 1991 and 1992, Architekturmuseum (Frankfurt) 1992, International Metropolitan Architects (Taipei) 1992, Universidad Menémdez Pelayo (Santander) 1993, Terzo Mileno (Comune di Rimini) 1993, Instituto Technológico de Monterrey (Mexico) 1994, Interior & Design Organization (Taipei) 1995, and Rotterdamse Kunststichting (Rotterdam) 1995, and Royal Institute of British Architects (London) 1995

(London) 1991 und 1992, Architekturmuseum (Frankfurt) 1992, International Metropolitan Architects (Taipeh) 1992, Universidad Menéndez Pelayo (Santander) 1993, Terzo Milenio (Rimini) 1993, Instituio Tecnológico de Monterrey (Mexico) 1994, Interior & Design Organization (Taipeh) 1995, Rotterdamse Kunststichting (Niederlande) 1995, Royal Institute of British Architects (London) 1995.

COOPERATORS

Marugame Hirai Contemporary Art Museum and Office Building, 1991-1993
Architect: Alfredo Arribas • Japanese Co-architects: Shimizu Architects & Engineers • Collaborators in Architecture: Miguel Morte, Pedro Luis Rocha, Luis Felipe Orozco, Martha Fonseca • Model: Nelson Cabello, Ramiro del Llano • Location: Marugame, Siko-ku, Japan • Photos: Nacasa & Partners

Hung Kuo Building – Shopping Mall and Residential Towers, 1994
Architects: Alfredo Arribas, Simon Chang • Chinese Co-architects: International Metropolitan Architects Taipei and Shanghai Office • Engineers: CEA • Collaborators in Architecture: Pedro Luis Rocha, Susan Mortimer, Cinthia Raccagni, Luis Felipe Orozco, Jordi Mercadé, Sergi Marimon • Location: Shanghai, China • Photos of the Model: Rafael Vargas

Gran Velvet – Multi-Use Leisure Space, 1991-1993
Architects: Alfredo Arribas, Miguel Morte • Engineers: IDOM • Collaborators in Architecture: Jordi Miró, Susan Mortimer, Adrián Mallol, Pedro Luis Rocha, Martha Fonseca, Sergi Marimon • Location: Montigalà, Badalona, Spain • Photos: Duccio Malagamba, Hisao Suzuki, Rafael Vargas

MCC Micro Compact Car – Sales Centers for European Cities, 1995
Architects: Alfredo Arribas, Marcià Codinachs, Miguel Morte • Structural Engineers: Robert Brufau • Installations/Service Consultants: Instalacions Arquitectòniques • Planning/Cost Estimation: Carles Romea • Collaborators in Architecture: Susan Mortimer, Pedro Luis Rocha, Adrián Mallol, Luis Felipe Orozco, Cinthia Raccagni, Xavier Dietz, Marta Soriano • Models: Jordi Aymerich, Jorge Moreno, Ramiro del Llano • Computer Images/Audiovisuals: Lluís Doménech, Carles Cabellos, Toni Alonso, Toni Farré, Carles Ellas, David Muñoz, Ivan Guardiola • Audiovisual Production: Xavier Ferrer

Estandard – Bar, Restaurant, Club, 1991-1993
Architect: Alfredo Arribas • Collaborators in Architecture: Miguel Morte, Pedro Luis Rocha, Alex Verdaguer, Daniel Goldschmid, Susana Thomas • Model: Nelson Cabello, Ramiro del Llano • Location: Travessera de Gràcia n. 39, Barcelona, Spain • Photos: Rafael Vargas, Duccio Malagamba

Medinaceli Palace for a Shipping Company – Offices Renewal, 1990-1994
Architects: Alfredo Arribas, Miguel Morte • Collaborators in Architecture: Martin Buchner, Nelson Cabello, Marta Soriano, Xavier Dietz • Location: Plaça Duc de Medinaceli n. 8, Barcelona, Spain • Photos: Rafael Vargas

Cosmo Hall Ceremony Halls – Buffet Restaurant, 1994-1995
Architects: Alfredo Arribas, Miguel Morte • Collaborators in Architecture: Susan Mortimer, Adrián Mallol, Xavier Dietz, Cinthia Raccagni • Model: Jordi Aymerich • Location: 48th and 49th floor of the World Trade Center, Osaka, Japan • Photos: Nacasa & Partners

Eurotower – Commercial Hall, Food Court, Glass House and Garden, 1995-1996
Architect: Alfredo Arribas • German Co-architects: HPP International • Collaborators in Architecture: Miguel Morte, Pedro Luis Rocha, Adrián Mallol, Ellen Rapelius, Alex Cazurra, Marta Soriano, Ellen Monge, Susan Mortimer • Models: Jordi Aymerich, Andrea Sacchi, Jorge Moreno • Location: Frankfurt am Main, Germany • Photos of the Model: Rafael Vargas

Furniture Elements
Sputnik Stool, 1992 • Designer: Alfredo Arribas • Producer: Ediciones llimitadas • *Torna Stool*, 1992 • Designer: Alfredo Arribas • Producer: Ediciones llimitadas • *Torna Llum Table*, 1994 • Designer: Alfredo Arribas • Producer: Ediciones llimitadas • *Zenio Ashtray*, 1992 • Designer: Alfredo Arribas • Producer: bd Ediciones de Diseño • *Fregoli Chair*, 1995 • Designer: Alfredo Arribas • Producer: Sawaya & Moroni • *Bola Sofa*, 1994 • Designer: Alfredo Arribas • Producer: Casas • *Copa Stool*, 1994 • Designer: Alfredo Arribas • Producer: Casas • *Pila Chair and Armchair*, 1995 • Designer: Alfredo Arribas • Producer: Casas • *Una Chair*, 1995 • Designer: Alfredo Arribas • Producer: Amat